The Ghosts of Detention (aka The Wedgie Club)

By

D. M. Larson

The Ghosts of Detention (aka The Wedgie Club)

Setting: 1980's High School Detention and Drama Club

See end of script for Cast of Characters

ACT I SCENE 1 - I NEED DETENTION

                    JIMMY
          I need detention. I really
          need detention. See, there's this
          girl... I know, I know, it always
          starts with a girl ... But this
          girl is special... I mean it this
          time... Really special. Her name
          is Harmony... But she goes my
          Harm. Cute huh? She can harm me
          any time she wants. And she has
          too. A couple of times. But I
          deserved it... Cause I touched her
          once. I didn't touch her anywhere
          bad. Just on the shoulder. And she
          broke my finger. So I guess we
          kind of have held hands. I was
          just gonna ask to borrow a
          pencil. One of those ones she
          sharpens with her pocket knife and
          then throws in the ceiling all over
          school. She even got one in the
          gym ceiling. You know how high
          that is? Like 5000 feet. And I
          just stand under those pencils,
          hoping one will fall down and I can
          have one of them for my very
          own. Something to remember her
          by. Until I get in to
          detention. I gotta figure out some
          way to get detention because I
          wanna see her more... Be with her
          more... And turn Harm into Harmony
          again... Cause I see that beautiful
          harmony under all that black and
          gloom. She just needs a reason to
          smile and I want to be that reason.
          So I have to get detention. What's
          something good... I mean I want it
          to be really, really good so I get
          thrown in there for a long time...
          Plus I have to make it worth it...
          Something great that she can
          respect... How about giving the
                    (MORE)

                                        (CONTINUED)

                         JIMMY (cont'd)
          principal a wedgie? That would do
          it... A good old up the back over
          the head mega wedgie. Let's do
          this.

THE GIRL WHO BROKE HIS FINGER

(HARM wears all black and is sharpening a pencil with a
pocket knife)

                         HARM
          I don't like to be touched... By
          anyone... Ever.

          Touch me and I touch you back...
          With my fist.

          I want to hurt them... Cause them
          pain like they did to me...
          Suffer... Squirm... Beg for mercy.

          This guy touched me... with a big
          smile on his face... Like he did it
          to be funny... And I broke his
          finger...

          Back in detention again for it... I
          wonder how long they can keep me in
          there... I must've racked up a few
          years by now... At the rate I'm
          going, I will 30 before I get out
          of high school detention.

          What's the point of trying... no
          point in being good and pretending
          because it never gets me
          anywhere... I've stopped wishing
          I'm something, I'm not.

WISHING

(PENNY is the school drama leading lady)

                         PENNY
          Have you ever made a wish? I make
          them all the time. I watch for the
          first star each night...

                         (MORE)

                                             (CONTINUED)

                              PENNY (cont'd)
          "Star light star bright, first star
          I see tonight... I wish I may, I
          wish I might, have the wish I wish
          tonight..." I always make the same
          wish, but I can't tell what it is.
          Then it might not come true. I
          really want it to. It would change
          my life.

          I go to wishing wells with lucky
          pennies... Those pennies you find
          that people have lost... Unlucky
          for them... Lucky for me... Then I
          toss them in the wishing well in
          front of the old museum.

          And I toss them in the fountain at
          the mall... Each time making my
          wish.

          Have you ever wanted anything that
          badly in your life? So badly that
          you can't imagine your future
          without it?

          I would be so sad if my life
          weren't different... If things
          didn't change... If I was still
          stuck here... In this life. But I
          won't stop wishing... I can't...

          I don't want to be left with
          nothing... zero... give me some
          meaning... and make this suffering
          worth while.

BIG ZERO

(Someone runs out in local team colors with a big "O"
painted on his chest (or stomach). A sports jersey with a
big "O" can work as well. He can have one of those giant
foam hands that he waves around. He is excited and screams
as he runs on the stage:)

                              BIFF
          Go team! Yeah!!!!!

(He calms down and smiles at the audience)
          Was that good? I'm practicing for
          the big game.

                                                     (CONTINUED)

(He looks at his O on his chest)
>   No, I'm not a zero. I am the O in
>   go team. Maybe I am a zero to some
>   people.
>
>   But this is my life. This is
>   something that matters to
>   me. Matters to me more than most
>   anything. You know why?
>
>   Unlike most things, there is a
>   clear start and finish.
>
>   There are heroes and villains.
>   Winners and losers. There's no
>   pretenders or double agents or
>   false friends. The uniforms make it
>   clear and simple. We know who to
>   root for and who to trust.
>
>   If only life were this simple...
>   This easy... good and bad... Right
>   and wrong.
>
>   What if war could be settled with a
>   game?
>
>   All the world problems - solved on
>   a Sunday.
>
>   Once a year we can have China vs
>   USA... India vs Pakistan... Winner
>   gets what they want for a year.
>
>   No more bombs and no more guns...
>   Just helmets and balls. It sure
>   would be a lot better than what
>   happens now. Because everyone who
>   fights a war is just a big zero.

UNDERDOG

(BENDER is staring at some good looking girls and grabs TINY as he comes by)

>   BENDER
> Fight me.
>
>   TINY
> I don't want to...

(BENDER punches TINY)

(CONTINUED)

                            TINY (CONT.)
                    Ow! What did you do that for?

                            BENDER
                    Plenty more where that came from...

(BENDER tries several more punches as TINY uses some folders
and papers as a shield)

                            TINY
                    Cut it out!

                            BENDER
                    Bet you're not so tough without
                    your shield, Captain America.

(BENDER slaps down folders, TINY yelps and BENDER tries a
few more punches)

                            TINY
                    Have you gone crazy?

                            BENDER
                    Something like that.

                            TINY
                    I won't fight you.

                            BENDER
                    Then I win.

                            TINY
                    Huh?

                            BENDER
                    I win.

                            TINY
                    I guess so.

(BENDER says loudly so girls hear him)

                            BENDER
                    Tell me I win.

                            TINY
                    Fine, you win.

(BENDER punches him)

                            BENDER
                    Louder.

(CONTINUED)

                         TINY
              You win!

                         BENDER
              That's right. I am the alpha dog,
              baby!

(BENDER does a chest bump against TINY who stumbles back)

                         TINY
              What is with you, man?

(BENDER grabs TINY in a headlock)

                         BENDER
              See her over there?

                         TINY
              Yolanda?

                         BENDER
              That her name? Yeah the new
              one. Yolanda... so hot.

                         TINY
              She's why you're acting like an
              idiot?

(BENDER stops headlock)

                         BENDER
              Yup... I want to impress her.

(BENDER lets TINY out of headlock)

                         TINY
              Great... Glad I could help.

                         BENDER
              She saw the whole thing. They're
              laughing. They think I am awesome.
              Now for the kill.

(TINY flinches)

                         BENDER (CONT.)
              Not you... Her. Gonna seal the
              deal.

(BENDER exits. TINY tries to fix himself up and gather
papers. BENDER returns and holds out a piece of paper)

                         TINY
          What's this?

                         BENDER
          Her number. She wants me to give it
          to you.

(Says it snotty)

                         BENDER (CONT.)
          She thought you were cute.

(BENDER walks off in defeat)

                         BENDER (CONT.)
          Everyone roots for the underdog.

(TINY looks at number happily and does a cute little wave)

THE USUAL SUSPECTS

(Some of the students from previous scenes [JIMMY, HARM,
PENNY, BIFF and BENDER] all standing in a row like a police
line up [i.e. The Usual Suspects movie poster])

(PRINCIPAL enters adjusting his pants in the rear. He throws
a detention slip at each of them as he walks by them
saying:)

                         PRINCIPAL
          Detention... detention...
          detention... detention....

(When he gets to JIMMY he gets an angry look and throws
multiple detention slips at him)

                         PRINCIPAL (CONT.)
          Detention, detention, detention.

(Principal goes out adjusting the rear of his pants and HARM
gives JIMMY a little smile when he isn't looking at her)

COACHES

(JIMMY, HARM, PENNY, BIFF and BENDER are all in
detention. More students can be included if desired. They
can be sitting or standing as COACH talks to them)

                                                  (CONTINUED)

                         COACH
          All right, losers. It must be your
          birthday because I am out of here.
          Your worst nightmare will soon be a
          memory... You have a new detention
          supervisor.

(GERTRUDE [drama teacher] pokes her head in)

                         GERTRUDE
          Introduce me like I said.

                         COACH
          I'm not doing any of that drama
          crap for you. Get your backside in
          here.

                         GERTRUDE
          Salutations children!

                         BENDER
          Ah! Not her. This is worse than
          coach.

                         COACH
          I'm out of here.

                         GERTRUDE
          Wait a minute, mister... You don't
          get away that easily. Even though
          this is a required timeout for all
          of you, I am sure some of you must
          have bonded with coach... Mr. Firm
          but Fair.

                         COACH
          Firm but not so fair I'd say...
          They lost their right to fair.

(GERTRUDE giggles)

                         GERTRUDE
          You say the funniest things.
          ...what I want everyone to do is
          introduce yourselves and then say
          one nice thing about coach...

                         HARM
          This is worse than torture.

                         COACH
          Any of you dare say anything nice
          about me then you'll get extra
                         (MORE)

                                              (CONTINUED)

                  COACH (cont'd)
detention because that means I
wasn't hard enough on
you. Detention is about
suffering...

                  GERTRUDE
It is about renewal and a second
chance.

                  COACH
It is about discipline.

                  GERTRUDE
Hope.

                  COACH
Agony.

                  GERTRUDE
Change.

                  COACH
Yeah a change of shorts because I
scared the you know what out of
you.

(COACH and GERTRUDE laugh)

                  GERTRUDE
You are so funny. Isn't he funny
children? You will be missed.

                  COACH
I doubt it. See you around,
Gertrude...

(This is an optional action depending on the age and
maturity of your actors and audience: COACH gives her butt a
slap as he leaves)

                  COACH
They're all yours!

                  GERTRUDE
You can call me, Gerty.

(GERTRUDE is embarrassed and does a cute little wave goodbye
and watches him go a little too long. Students chuckle)

                  GERTRUDE
I have some wonderful news for all
of you. Instead of your usual
                (MORE)

(CONTINUED)

                    GERTRUDE (cont'd)
          detention I have an amazing growth
          opportunity for you. We will be
          performing a play! One of the
          challenges with school drama is
          finding a large cast for some of
          the plays we would like to do. So
          all of you will be taking parts in
          our next production. If you
          successfully complete the entire
          production, then you get released
          from detention. But who knows...
          Some of you might get bit by the
          theatre bug.

                    HARM
          I'd rather get bit by something
          that would make me dead.

                    JIMMY
          Good one, Harm.

(JIMMY laughs a little too hard at her joke. She punches
him in the arm and he stops)

                    GERTRUDE
          Just like a couple of my star
          performers... There is Penny
          Hepburn of course... one of your
          fellow students here.

(PENNY stands and does a little bow. GERTRUDE claps
happily)

                    GERTRUDE (CONT.)
          And last but not least, presenting
          our future star of stage and
          screen... Brad Gable!

(BRAD comes in dramatically. PENNY and GERTRUDE clap and
cheer. BRAD does dramatic bows and waves and blows kisses
to PENNY and GERTRUDE)

                    BRAD
          Thank you everyone. I am here to
          guide you not only on the stage but
          on this actor's journey to the
          soul. Drama is everything to
          me. As an actor, I want to leave
          my mark. I want to make a
          difference. In this school, they
          worship the quarterback and collect
          lots of sports trophies. I want to
                    (MORE)

                                          (CONTINUED)

                         BRAD (cont'd)
          change all that. I want to give
          this school a drama trophy. I want
          to win best actor at the state
          drama competition. I want this
          school to be proud of their amazing
          actors. I want to stand in front
          of you and proudly say I am Best in
          Show.

                         BENDER
          That's for sure.

(BENDER barks at him)

                         BRAD
          Oh! A method actor.

(BRAD barks back at him)

                         GERTY
          Oh, you dogs.

(BRAD laughs at her joke. BENDER growls)

                         GERTRUDE (CONT.)
          This is so exciting. The play we
          are going to do is a 1920's tale of
          murder and mystery. It was time of
          flappers, prohibition and
          gangsters. I thought this might be
          good since some of you kids in
          detention might be from gangs. Do
          we have any real gangsters among
          you that could help make this
          authentic for us?

(The students laugh and chuckle)

                         BENDER
          You want us to be from one of them
          gangs that kills people or just
          that steals stuff?

(BENDER'S question makes GERTRUDE and BRAD very
nervous. They look at each other confused)

                         GERTRUDE
          Uh... Well... I'm not sure ...
          We'll just figure that out as we
          go.

                        HARM
          So why should we do all this for
          you? What if we refuse? We're in
          detention already. How you going
          to make it worse?

                        GERTRUDE
          Some of you are the worst detention
          offenders but I promise you time
          off for good behavior. Doing well
          in my production means an early
          ticket out of detention.

                        BENDER
          Is it a musical? Need any
          singers? I can sing. 99 bottles
          of beer on the wall, 99 bottles of
          beer, take one down, pass it
          around... 98 bottles of beer on the
          wall.

                        BRAD
          Hey, I know that one.

(BRAD starts to join BENDER but BENDER stops)

                        JIMMY
          Are there any parts with kissing?

(JIMMY glances at HARM who isn't paying attention)

                        GERTRUDE
          Yes, there will be some kissing.

(HARM makes a gagging motion and sound. BENDER makes kissy
sounds at PENNY)

                        GERTRUDE (CONT.)
          Brad and I are going to step out a
          moment and discuss some of the
          casting. Please remain in your
          assigned spots. We'll be close by
          so no funny business.

(GERTRUDE and BRAD exit and BENDER immediately gets out of
his chair and starts wandering the room. He stops at PENNY)

                        BENDER
          So, it's bad Penny... always
          turning up. Why you in here drama
          queen?

                    PENNY
          I did nothing. I'm innocent.

                    BENDER
          I heard you did something pretty
          bad. You stole something from the
          principal. You broke in his office
          and took something. What was it?

(Other students turn and listen)

                    PENNY
          The crown jewels. Or the Hope
          diamond. I can't remember
          which. I steal so much I lose
          track.

                    BENDER
          I'm starting to like you drama
          queen.

                    PENNY
          Too bad.

                    BENDER
          What was it, Penny? Come on.

                    PENNY
          It was helping out a friend. Now
          drop it, okay?

                    BIFF
          Leave her alone, Bender.

(BENDER goes to BIFF)

                    BENDER
          If it isn't our head
          cheerleader? Here is cheer us up
          in detention? I always thought it
          was a little weird a guy wanted to
          be a cheerleader. I mean, maybe a
          mascot, so you can hide your
          face... although our mascot is the
          woodchuck, so that can't be too
          cool. Why you in here cheerboy?

                    BIFF
          I beat up somebody... punched his
          face in... Got tired of him saying
          certain thing about me that wasn't
          true.

BENDER
I bet we know what he was saying,
Cheerboy. We all think it but he
was the only one stupid enough to
say it.

BIFF
Well, I'm not.

(BIFF slams down his fist on a desk or table. BENDER backs
off. He makes his way over to HARM. He tries to touch HARM
and she hits his hand away. JIMMY gets worried)

BENDER
What's the matter? You don't want
to be my girlfriend anymore?

HARM
I never was, loser.

BENDER
That hurts. I thought we had
something.

(BENDER is about to touch her again)

HARM
Touch me again and die.

BENDER
Just one little kiss?

(JIMMY grabs BENDER)

JIMMY
Leave her alone.

(BENDER turns slowly and towers over JIMMY)

BENDER
You say something?

JIMMY
Yeah... leave her... alone.

BENDER
Make me.

(JIMMY gives BENDER a shove. BENDER laughs and goes to
attack JIMMY. JIMMY ducks and BENDER is grabbed by
BIFF. BIFF, HARM and JIMMY all grab BENDER and shove him in
a closet [can be off stage])

(CONTINUED)

                         BENDER (CONT.)
          Hey, hey... what are you doing?

(They all return happily to their desks)

                         BENDER (CONT.)
          Let me out of here.

                         BIFF
          Nice one, Jimmy.

                         JIMMY
          Thanks.

(HARM gives a little smile at JIMMY who is very happy she
noticed. PENNY pulls some stuff out of her backpack)

                         PENNY
          Anyone like JOLT cola?

                         BIFF
          Oh, yeah. That stuff makes me
          bounce off the walls.

                         PENNY
          I like to add pop rocks to it.

(PENNY opens a can and pours some pop rocks in)

                         BIFF
          Awesome.

(BIFF drinks it)

                         BIFF (CONT.)
          Oh, yeah!

(JIMMY goes over and tries it)

                         JIMMY
          Ha! This is too much.

(PENNY takes one over to HARM)

                         PENNY
          Want one?

(HARM shrugs. PENNY gives her one. HARM tries it and slaps
her nose)

                         PENNY (CONT.)
          Oh yeah... it comes out your nose
          sometimes.

(PENNY tries to hold in a laugh but BIFF and JIMMY can't
help but laugh)

                    BENDER (OFF)
          What about me? I want one.

(JIMMY gets an unopened can and shakes it. They
laugh. JIMMY goes and tosses it quickly in the closet)

                    JIMMY
          There you go.

                    BENDER
          Thanks, man.

(He opens it and they hear it explode. They laugh)

                    BENDER (CONT.)
          Not funny.

(NOTE: Optional scene - They put on some music and do a
dance together)

                    END OF SCENE

ACT I SCENE 2 MEET MADELINE AND JASMINE

SONG with MADELINE (NOTE: songs are optional)

The house is haunted By the echo of your last goodbye

The house is haunted By the memories that refuse to die

I can't get away from the vision that brings

Intimate glimpses of intimate things

A voice in my heart like a torch singer sings I wonder who's
kissing her now.

The house is haunted By the echo of your favourite song

The place is cluttered up With roses that have lived too
long

Much too long The ceiling is white but the shadows are black

A ghost in my heart says You'll never come back

The house is haunted By the echo of your last goodbye.

ANOTHER SONG OPTION:

I FOUND A ROSE IN THE DEVIL'S GARDEN

Willy Raskin / Fred Fisher, 1921

Lost in a city that has no pity I found a rose, Little
lonesome rose; Where smiling faces, hide broken hearts, In
happy places, where sorrow starts:

Some body's sister, whose folks have missed her, A mother
dear, She's a lonesome tear; For little baby, who went away,
She's kneeling maybe, just now to pray:

I found a rose, in the devil's garden, Wandring alone,
little lonesome rose, For her the sun is never shining, For
her the clouds have, no silver lining I found a rose, in the
devil's garden, Playing the game, of the Moth and Flame,
Beneath the powder and paint, Maybe the heart of a saint,
Where sorrow grows, I found a rose.

I found a rose, in the devil's garden, Wandring alone,
little lonesome rose, For her the sun is never shining, For
her the clouds have, no silver lining I found a rose, in the
devil's garden, Playing the game, of the Moth and Flame, But
maybe deep in her heart, She's thinking of a new start,
Where sorrow grows, I found a rose.

(GERTY and BRAD re-enter)

                    GERTY
          Everyone... meet, Madeline. She
          will be playing the part of Maya,
          the mysterious mystic who can speak
          with the dead.

                    MADELINE
          Hello, everyone.

                    BENDER
          Can I call you Mad or Maddy or
          something?

                    MADELINE
          You can call me Maya. I plan on
          staying in character for the entire
          rehearsal process.

                    BENDER
          So you gonna read are fortunes and
          stuff?

                    MADELINE
          And read your mind.

                                            (CONTINUED)

                         BENDER
          Really?

                         MADELINE
          Yeah and the answer's no.

(Other students laugh at him)

                         GERTRUDE
          We have your parts picked out
          everyone. Penny is going to play
          Remmy who is the woman who has
          found herself in debt to the Capone
          family and seeks help to get free
          from their evil clutches.

                         PENNY
          So she's kind of the damsel in
          distress?

                         GERTRUDE
          Exactly. Brad will be playing Pete
          the detective who has a plan to
          stop Cal Capone.

                         JIMMY
          Don't you mean Al?

                         GERTRUDE
          Al is in this but the main bad guy
          is Cal, his brother.

                         JIMMY
          Did Al have a brother?

                         GERTRUDE
          I don't know... I guess so... but
          this is a made up story... so maybe
          not.

                         BENDER
          I wanna be Cal. I wanna be the bad
          guy. Where's my machine gun?

(BENDER pretends to have a machine gun and makes machine gun
noises)

                         HARM
          Grow up, Bender. What are you...
          like 8?

                    GERTRUDE
          Well, Mr. Bender... you're in luck
          because you will be playing Cal
          Capone.

                    BENDER
          Score!

(BENDER makes more machine gun noises)

                    GERTRUDE
          Harmony... you'll be playing
          Remmy's friend Flo.

                    PENNY
          That's cool.

(PENNY gives HARM a thumbs up and HARM shrugs)

                    GERTRUDE
          Jimmy. You'll be playing several
          roles including the famous bad guy
          Al Capone.

                    JIMMY
          Is that because I have a split
          personality?

                    GERTUDE
          Uh... you do?

                    JIMMY
          No, just kidding... no, I'm not...
          yes, you are... Me, myself and I
          are ready.

(HARM rolls her eyes but thinks it's kind of funny)

                    GERTRUDE
          Biff. You'll play Jaque... he's
          Maya the psychic's ghost hunting
          partner but also is tied up in a
          relationship with the evil, two
          faced woman named Vera.

                    BIFF
          Dang... sounds like I got my work
          cut out for me.

                    PENNY
          Who's playing the vamp, Vera?

                          GERTRUDE
          I still need to find someone.

                          HARM
          How about Bender's mom?

                          BENDER
          Can she be in the play?

                          HARM
          That was an insult, idiot.

                          BENDER
          Whatever.

                          BRAD
          So when are we going to start, Mrs.
          Fenstermacher?

                          GERTRUDE
          You're such an eager beaver, Brad.

                          BENDER
          Oh, hey, Brad... can we call you
          Beaver?

                          BRAD
          A nickname? Sure! I've never had
          a nickname.

                          BENDER
          Okay, Beaver.

(He laughs and sticks his front teeth out like a beaver and
Brad joins him in laughing)

                          GERTRUDE
          You're in luck, Brad...

                          BRAD
          Beaver.

                          GERTRUDE
          Okay... Beaver. We will practice
          our first scene today.

(PENNY, MADELINE and BRAD are excited. The rest sigh and
roll their eyes except for BENDER who does mock excitement,
clapping his hands like an excited little girl)

                          BRAD
          Can I be in it?

> GERTRUDE
> Yes, Beaver... you're character's
> in it. Along with Madeline, Biff
> and Jimmy.

(NOTE: If other actors are available, JIMMY and BIFF's parts
in this scene [Detective 2 and Henry] can be played by other
actors)

> GERTRUDE
> Here are your scripts. Biff...
> this is not your main character...
> this is one of the other characters
> you'll play. Henry is one of the
> crime partners who worked with
> Bonnie and Clyde. The scene is a
> flashback to when Pete the
> Detective and Maya the Psychic once
> worked together.

> JIMMY
> I thought Bonnie and Clyde died
> after Al Capone when to jail?

> GERTRUDE
> Well, aren't you the walking
> encyclopedia? How about we allow
> the author of this play some
> artistic license?

> JIMMY
> Okay. I guess. I mean... it might
> bother the audience. I think
> everyone knows Bonnie and Clyde
> died in 1934 and Al Capone went to
> jail in 1931.

> HARM
> Holy cow crap... how did you know
> that?

> JIMMY
> I love history and seem to memorize
> dates easily.

> HARM
> When did Jim Morrison die?

> JIMMY
> July 3, 1971.

                              HARM
                    Jimi Hendrix?

                              JIMMY
                    September 18, 1970.

                              HARM
                    That's incredible. Well, that's
                    all history I know. Anyone else
                    want to try?

                              GERTRUDE
                    This is drama, not history. Shall
                    we continue everyone?

                              HARM
                    You totally need to go on Jeopardy,
                    Jimmy.

(JIMMY is really happy HARM noticed him. GERTRUDE has to
poke him a couple of times to get him to take his script.
She hands out scripts to everyone and BRAD and MADELINE set
up the scene - a chair, a table and lamp that can be pointed
in HENRY's face. The lights go out for total darkness and
then the lamp snaps on and HENRY [played by BIFF or another
actor] is in the chair looking nervous. PETE and JIMMY as
DETECTIVES appear. MADELINE is now MAYA the psychic)

BONNIE AND CLYDE

(A couple of 1930's detectives are in a room with a table
with a nicely dressed criminal. There is also an oddly
dressed woman in the room that is a MAYA)

                         DETECTIVE 1 / PETE
                    All right, you. I'm gonna give you
                    one more chance to spill the beans
                    or we're gonna toss you in the
                    slammer and throw away the key.

                         DETECTIVE 2 / JIMMY
                    Easy there, detective. Henry here
                    is ready to tell us all about
                    Bonnie and Hyde.

                              HENRY
                    Clyde.

                         DETECTIVE 2
                    See. He's very cooperative.

                                                      (CONTINUED)

                    HENRY
And what are you going to do if I
don't spill the beans?

                    DETECTIVE 1
Then this psychic here, Madame
Maya, is gonna read your mind.

                    HENRY
So what do you want to know?

                    DETECTIVE 2
What was Clyde's real name? I have
here a series aliases: Roy Bailey,
Jack Hale, Eldin Williams, Elvin
Williams and Donald the Duck.

                    HENRY
His real name was Clyde Barrow.

                    DETECTIVE 1
What was his middle name?!

                    HERNY
I don't remember!

                    MAYA
He liked to go by Tiberius but it
was actually Chestnut.

                    HENRY
Hey, I think that's right. Maybe
you should ask her all the
questions.

                    DETECTIVE 1
Don't get smart with me.

                    DETECTIVE 2
So what was Clyde like as a kid?

                    HENRY
He stole jalopies and took them for
joy rides.

                    DETECTIVE 2
So what was Clyde's first crime?

                    HENRY
He and Bonnie robbed a bank in
Missouri and got away with $115.

                         DETECTIVE 1
          That's it?

                         HENRY
          The banks don't have much money
          anymore. It's the Great Depression
          remember?

                         DETECTIVE 2
          True.

                         DETECTIVE 1
          We know he was bank robber. Didn't
          he also take hostages and torture
          them?

                         HENRY
          Well, there was this one time he
          kidnapped a cop and made him steal
          a car battery and install it before
          we let him go.

                         DETECTIVE 1
          He also killed 13 people!

                         HENRY
          I don't know if it was that many.

                         MAYA
          It was more like six.

                         HENRY
          Look. I told you everything I know.
          I helped you find them. Aren't I
          free to go?

                         DETECTIVE 1
          Well, you've been cleared of all
          your charges in Texas, but you're
          still wanted in Oklahoma for grand
          theft auto.

                         HENRY
          What? How long do I have to be in
          jail for stealing a car?

                         MAYA
          Twelve years and then when you get
          out you'll be hit by a train.

                         HENRY
          What?! Wait!

                         DETECTIVE 1
              Get him out of here.

(Detective 2 removes HENRY)

                         MAYA
              So how many people did you arrest
              for helping Bonnie and Clyde?

                         DETECTIVE 1
              Twenty-three.

                         MAYA
              Twenty-three! Are you sure?

                         DETECTIVE 1
              Yes, why?

                         MAYA
              Did you know Bonnie was 23 when she
              was killed? And they were killed
              on May 23.

                         DETECTIVE 1
              You're right!

                         MAYA
              Of course I'm right. And out of
              167 bullets fired. 50 hit Bonnie
              and Clyde... 23 of those just hit
              Bonnie.

                         DETECTIVE 1
              Now, now. I don't know about that.

                         MAYA
              And she had twenty-three pennies in
              her purse at her time of death.

                         DETECTIVE 1
              Get her out of here.

(Detective 2 comes in and drags out MAYA)

                         DETECTIVE 1 (CONT.)
              Dang, now she has me curious. I'm
              gonna have to go look in her purse.

                         END OF SCENE

(Everyone claps and the cast from the scene bows, especially
BRAD)

                          BENDER
              Way to go, Beaver!

(JASMINE runs in nervously)

                          JASMINE
              Oh, no... I'm late... I'm so sorry
              I'm late... I didn't mean to
              interrupt.

                          GERTRUDE
              That's okay, my dear. We still
              need some more actors. There's the
              evil, vamp named Vera. And also,
              the ghost named Sadie who was the
              one who was... murdered!

                          BRAD
              Oh! You scared me with the way you
              said that... say it again.

                          GERTRUDE
              Murdered!

                          BRAD
              Eeek! Again!

(PENNY stops them before they get too carried away)

                          PENNY
              So yes... please join us... we need
              more actors.

                          JASMINE
              Oh, good. I have my monologue
              prepared. I'm ready to audition.

                          GERTRUDE
              How professional. Make note
              everyone. She is prepared to
              audition with a monologue.

                          BENDER
              What's a monologue? Does it
              involve a toilet?

                          GERTRUDE
              How crude, Mr. Bender. I'd send
              you to detention for that but
              you're already there.

                         PENNY
          What's your name?

                         JASMINE
          Jasmine Jones.

                         PENNY
          Welcome, Jasmine.

                         GERTRUDE
          You may now perform your monologue
          for us.

                         JASMINE
          Okay... great... let me get in
          character.

(JASMINE puts on crown... she is a princess and can have on
a fancy costume dress too if desired. Everyone backs away
and she gets center stage)

                         JASMINE (AS PRINCESS)
          Okay, people. I wished upon a star.
          I guess it does make a difference
          who I are! Do I have to be some
          poor nobody wannabe? Do I need some
          kind of kryptonite like a little
          pea? Did my prince get turned into
          a frog and he's now hiding in some
          creepy bog waiting for me to find
          him? I don't even know how to swim.
          What's the use of dreaming anymore.
          No one is beating down my door. I
          need to be some kind of damsel in
          distress to get some attention I
          guess. Where's my Prince Charming?
          Is there something about me that's
          alarming? All I get is Prince
          Pampered who spends his whole life
          hampered by being royally stuck up.
          Or there's Prince Never Grow Up who
          is way too pretty in his curls. All
          these boys make me want to hurl.
          Why can't I find a man-sized prince
          who will sweep me off my feet and
          take me to far away lands. He will
          hold me with his strong hands and
          devote his life to me. Is that what
          I want? Is that what I dream about?
          If I don't get it, will I forever
          pout and cry because I didn't get
          my way?

                         (MORE)

                          JASMINE (AS PRINCESS) (cont'd)
          I just want to feel special. I want
          to feel like they care. I want them
          to bravely face any challenge for
          me. Enter my heart if you dare.
          Lock me in a tower. Make me your
          precious flower. I want you to
          battle your way against dragons to
          win my love today. Quit playing
          with your toys and prove your worth
          to me, boys. I promise I will be
          the perfect princess for you to
          please. I will be good to you and I
          won't be a tease... much. Who am I
          kidding? I'm chasing a dream. They
          say I got everything in life but it
          is nothing it seems. Where is my
          happy ending?!

(JASMINE bows her head showing she is finished. Everyone
claps for her)

                          GERTRUDE
          Bravo, Jasmine. Most excellent. I
          am going to have you play the role
          of the tortured spirit in our play,
          Sadie the ghost.

                          BENDER
          Casper's sister.

                          JASMINE
          That's wonderful. Thank you so
          much.

                          GERTRUDE
          Wonderful practice everyone. I
          have high hopes for this one.

                          BRAD
               (sings)
          High hopes... she's got high
          hopes...

(BRAD and GERTRUDE exit together singing)

                          BRAD AND GERTRUDE
          She's got high apple pie in the sky
          hopes...

                          JASMINE
          They're interesting.

                                                     (CONTINUED)

                              PENNY
                    You're telling me.

(The rest of the students exit except for BENDER and BIFF
who linger. BIFF motions for BENDER to beat it and he leaves
annoyed)

                              BIFF
                    Hey, Jasmine. That was great.

                              JASMINE
                    Oh, hey, Biff. I didn't know you
                    were doing the play too.

                              BIFF
                    I didn't really have a choice. I'm
                    one of the detention detainees that
                    has to do the play for a get out of
                    jail free card.

                              JASMINE
                    Is that why you had to quit
                    cheerleading?

                              BIFF
                    Yeah... plus I hit a football
                    player.

                              JASMINE
                    Yeah... that was kind of
                    funny. How many football players
                    get knocked out by cheerleaders?

                              BIFF
                    I guess it is kind of funny. So
                    you're not cheerleading anymore?

                              JASMINE
                    They cut me.

                              BIFF
                    What?

                              JASMINE
                    The new captain hates me.

                              BIFF
                    But you're awesome... I mean...
                    you're so much better than her.

                              JASMINE
                    That's the problem.

>   BIFF
> I'll talk to her if you want.

>   JASMINE
> No, that's okay. I want to try
> drama now.

>   BIFF
> That's cool.

>   JASMINE
> Yeah... and even better that there
> is a friend here too.

>   BIFF
> Right on.

(They have a quiet, shy, awkward moment)

>   BIFF (CONT.)
> So you... uh... are still looking
> for your Prince Charming?

>   JASMINE
> What? Oh! The monologue... yeah, I
> guess so. I picked the monologue
> because that's how I feel
> sometimes. Where's my Prince
> Charming? Where's my happy ending?
> You see all those movies and wonder
> why all our lives can't be that
> way. I keep waiting for that movie
> moment where everything turns
> around for me... where something
> amazing happens... or someone
> amazing comes along and sweeps me
> off my feet.

>   BIFF
> Yeah. You were great... with the
> monologue... I really believed you
> were some princess. Very cool.

>   JASMINE
> Thanks... I practiced it a lot. I
> wanted to be good.

>   BIFF
> You always are... I mean you always
> did your best with
> cheerleading. You always had all
> the routines down first. I always
> counted on you to help the others.

                          JASMINE
          You were an awesome captain.
          Very... inspiring.

(Quiet, shy moment again)

                          JASMINE
          So Biff?

                          BIFF
          Yeah?

                          JASMINE
          Can I ask you something personal?

                          BIFF
          Sure... shoot.

                          JASMINE
          Is what that football player
          said... was any of it true?

                          BIFF
          Nope, not a word.

                          JASMINE
          So you're not...

                          BIFF
          No...

                          JASMINE
          Cool.

                          BIFF
          Really?

                          JASMINE
          Oh... uh... I better go...

                          BIFF
          Okay.

                          JASMINE
          See you at drama practice tomorrow!

                          BIFF
          Totally!

(JASMINE leaves and BIFF is very happy)

                                        (CONTINUED)

                            BIFF (CONT.)
               I think I just got bit by the
               theatre bug.

                            END OF SCENE

PRINCIPAL PAINE

(GERTRUDE is getting the stage ready for their first
performance. The PRINCIPAL enters)

                            PRINCIPAL
               Hello, Gertrude.

                            GERTRUDE
               Oh, goodness. You startled me,
               Principal Paine.

                            PRINCIPAL
               Is there any reason you're feeling
               jumpy? Something you're worried
               about?

                            GERTRUDE
               What does that mean?

                            PRINCIPAL
               I had an interesting little chat
               with our school secretary who just
               finished going through the file
               cabinets that were broken in to.

                            GERTRUDE
               The ones in your office?

                            PRINCIPAL
               It was interesting to me that it
               was only teacher personnel files
               that were taken.

                            GERTRUDE
               Oh?

                            PRINCIPAL
               Yours was one of them.

                            GERTRUDE
               Oh dear... do you suspect an
               identity theft kind of thing? I
               better call my bank or something...
               who do you call about identity
               theft?

                    PRINCIPAL
          Well... I'm trying to put all the
          pieces of the puzzle
          together. See, it was one of your
          drama students, Penny, who took the
          files.

                    GERTRUDE
          Yes, she is serving detention with
          me now.

                    PRINCIPAL
          And doing something for detention
          that she loves to do. Not much of
          a punishment.

                    GERTRUDE
          I'm being very hard on her.

                    PRINCIPAL
          I'm sure you are.

(PRINCIPAL walks about the stage looking at things. He
inspects a bottle and sniffs it)

                    GERTRUDE
          Principal Paine... I'm very busy
          getting ready for our performance
          tonight. Is there anything else on
          your mind you'd like to share with
          me?

                    PRINCIPAL
          Actually it's you who might want to
          share with me.

                    GERTRUDE
          I have no clue what you're talking
          about.

                    PRINCIPAL
          Very well. We'll do this the hard
          way. I shall continue my
          investigation and when I find out
          why YOUR student, Penny Hepburn,
          took YOUR file...

                    GERTRUDE
          And other files...

                    PRINCIPAL
          Then I will be back in touch with
          you. Don't leave town, Mrs.
          Fenstermacher.

                                        (CONTINUED)

(PRINCIPAL leaves and GERTRUDE sits very worried. The
students start arriving. Everyone is getting into costumes
and gathering props. PENNY sees GERTRUDE is upset and goes
to her)

                    PENNY
          Everything okay?

                    GERTRUDE
          Not really.

                    PENNY
          What's wrong?

                    GERTRUDE
          I got a visit from the Principal.

                    PENNY
          What did he say?

                    GERTRUDE
          He's on to me.

                    PENNY
          What? No. He can't be. How did he
          figure it out?

                    GERTRUDE
          He's not as dumb as he looks.

                    PENNY
          Maybe he's bluffing. Maybe he
          talked to all the teachers. You
          didn't tell him anything did you?

                    GERTRUDE
          No, but it's only a matter of time
          before he figures something
          out. And I'm going to get much
          worse than detention.

                    PENNY
          I'm so sorry.

                    GERTRUDE
          You did way more than you should
          have.

                    PENNY
          I feel bad that I messed things up
          for you.

                    GERTRUDE
          I didn't realize you were staying
          late working on the set. I thought
          I was alone in the school and could
          get in and out of the office
          without anyone seeing.

                    PENNY
          I thought there was someone
          breaking in the school. If I
          hadn't called the police...

                    GERTRUDE
          But then you turned yourself in and
          said it was you and I escaped...
          undetected... so we thought.

                    PENNY
          I tried...

                    GERTRUDE
          You did wonderfully... I never
          should have let you take the fall
          for me.

                    PENNY
          I'm a minor... it won't stay on my
          record like it would have for you.

                    GERTRUDE
          What a wonderful person you are...
          you dedication and devotion makes
          all this worth while. And look at
          these detention students. They all
          showed... they're all working hard
          to make this production a
          success. I think some of them are
          even enjoying detention.

                    PENNY
          A lot of them are. You've really
          made a difference.

                    GERTRUDE
          Music to my ears... that's what
          every teacher wants to hear. At
          least I'll go out with a bang.

                    PENNY
          This is so hard...

                    GERTRUDE
          Focus on the performance... the
          show must go on!

                  END OF SCENE

ACT 1 SCENE 3 - LONESOME SONG

(Song can be sung by PENNY AS REMMY or MADELINE AS MAYA)

When You're Good You're Lonesome - Song and Lyrics by Grace
Doro

First Verse I feel so sad and lonely I wish I knew just why
Every one is happy, While all I do is sigh. I walk the
straight and narrow path I'm good as I can be; Maybe that's
just what is wrong, For it seems to me.

Second Verse My mother always told me "Be very, very good;"
I took her advice, Like a good child always should. I went
to bed at eight o'clock But what did that get me? I have
missed an awful lot, Now I plainly see.

Chorus When you are good, you're so lonesome, And when
you're lonesome you're blue; Sometimes it seems very hard to
believe Every dark cloud has a silver lining I think it'll
get me a sweetie who'll make a fuss over me, Just love and
pet me all the day; Then I'll never have to say When you are
good you're so lonesome, And when you're lonesome you're
blue.

GHOST HUNTERS OF RT 666

(Lights come up on a room. There a few tables and chairs in
the room. REMMY, enters nervously and looks around)

                    REMMY
          Hello? Any ghosts in here?

(FLO follows REMMY in)

                    FLO
          So this is the place?

                    REMMY
          I think it will work for our little
          business.

                                      (CONTINUED)

                    FLO
A pickle factory.

                    REMMY
That's just a cover.

                    FLO
I know. I was trying to play along.

                    REMMY
This is out of the way but close
enough to the action.

                    FLO
I don't know if I want all that
action.

                    REMMY
I don't think we have a
choice. We've got debts to
pay. This is the only way to do it
quick enough for the Capones.

                    FLO
Stinkin' Capones. Help us then
ruin our lives for it.

                    REMMY
We do this, then we're done with
them. I promise.

                    FLO
You look spooked.

                    REMMY
They say this place is
haunted. That's why it's so cheap.

                    FLO
You can relax, Remmy. I think
the ghost busters are here.

                    REMMY
This isn't funny, Flo. Something
really bad happened here.

                    FLO
Paying money to have these guys
come and scare our ghosts is what's
funny.

(CONTINUED)

                         REMMY
               As long as they get rid of them,
               that's all I care about.

(First enters JAQUE. He is in a suit, slicked back hair, and
carries some electronic gadgetry.

JAQUE's device could look something like this:

http://freedramaplays.blogspot.com/2014/03/
upcoming-play-prop-flip-flop-circuit.html

MAYA follows. MAYA is flamboyantly dressed and looks around
at nothing like a cat. JAQUE is flipping switches to make
his device light up)

                         JAQUE
               I'm getting some strong readings
               here.

(MAYA rushes to him dramatically)

                         MAYA
               Let me see.
               (Looks)
               Yes, excellent. Exactly as I
               expected. THIS is the room.

                         FLO
               Brilliant. We already told her that
               on the way in.

                         REMMY
               Hush, Flo.

(JAQUE waves his gadget around and then points to a chair
that one of audience members is sitting in)

                         JAQUE
               The strongest readings are there.
               And there.

(JAQUE points to the ceiling above that table)

                         REMMY
               Oh, my gosh. He's right. The owner
               told me that too.

                         FLO
               Did you tell him that?

                                              (CONTINUED)

                         REMMY
          No, they haven't ever been in this
          room before.

                         MAYA
          Please tell us more of the history
          of this room. What do you know
          already about the ones who inhabit
          this place?

                         REMMY
          We don't know much at all actually.

                         FLO
          We wanted to buy this building
          because it is cheap.

                         REMMY
          The reason this building was so
          cheap was because past owners
          claimed it was haunted.

                         FLO
          I've never believed in that stuff
          so I thought what the heck. Let's
          get it.

                         REMMY
          Then strange things started to
          happen.

                         MAYA
          Things started to disappear?

     (REMMY is amazed)

                         REMMY
          Yes.

                         MAYA
          Objects would be in one place, then
          show up in another.

                         REMMY
          Exactly. How did you know?

                         MAYA
          That's usually how it starts.

                         FLO
          I didn't believe any of it though
          until that one night.

                                         (CONTINUED)

                              MAYA
              The night you'd never forget.

                              REMMY
              We drove by one night to discuss
              the place one last time before we
              bought it.

                              FLO
              I saw a light go on. I immediately
              thought burglars.

                              REMMY
              I told Flo we should call the
              police but she wanted to go in and
              scare them off herself. She ended
              up getting scared instead.

                              FLO
              I wouldn't say I was scared.

                              REMMY
              I would.

                              FLO
              Anyway, we got out of the car,
              pulled out the tire iron from the
              trunk and headed for the door. I
              froze when I saw...

(MAYA points fearfully at ceiling above the table mentioned
before)

                              MAYA
              A body hanging there...

(FLO is surprised)

                              FLO
              Yes.

(MAYA is starting to cry really hard)

                              MAYA
              And crying coming from that chair.

                              FLO
              Yes.

(MAYA falls into the chair)

                         MAYA
          Oh, John. John!!!

                         FLO
          Is she okay?

                         JAQUE
          Step back. She is picking up a
          presence. Look at these readings.
          They're off the chart.

(JAQUE holds up his gadget while he flips switches to make
the lights flash)

                         REMMY
          Are you sure this is safe?

                         JAQUE
          Completely.

(Crossing dramatically to MAYA)

                         JAQUE (CONT.)
          Spirit?

(MAYA just sobs)

                         JAQUE (CONT.)
          Spirit! Tell me you name!

                         MAYA
          Oh, John. Why? Why did you do this?

                         JAQUE
          John? Who is John?

                         MAYA
          I loved John. I loved him so much.

                         JAQUE
          What happened? What happened to
          John?

                         MAYA
          I want to die.

                         JAQUE
          Please, tell me what happened here.
          We want to help.

                         MAYA
          I want to die!

(MAYA runs for a knife on another table)

                                           (CONTINUED)

                    REMMY
          Look out! She's after the knife.

(JAQUE grabs MAYA as she grabs the knife)

                    JAQUE
          Spirit! Spirit be gone!

(MAYA drops the knife and then goes limp)

                    JAQUE
          Get her a chair.

(FLO rushes to get one and sits her in it)

                    REMMY
          Is she okay?

                    JAQUE
          When a spirit enters and leaves
          her, it drains her completely.

                    MAYA
               (Weakly)
          Jaque?

                    JAQUE
          Yes, Maya?

                    MAYA
          Check your instrument.

                    JAQUE
          What?

                    MAYA
          Check it, quick.

                    JAQUE
          I'm getting another reading.
          Different this time.

                    MAYA
          John? John, are you there? I hear
          him.

                    JAQUE
          What is he saying?

                    MAYA
          He says, he says... my neck hurts
          so bad.

                          JAQUE
          Strangulation, did he hang himself?

                          MAYA
          John? Did you hang yourself? I see.

                          REMMY
          What did he say?

                          MAYA
          He said that his love, Sadie, loved
          another.

                          REMMY
          But she sounded like she loved him
          to me.

                          MAYA
          John? Do you think it was a
          mistake? Some kind of
          misunderstanding? John. Listen to
          me. John!

                          REMMY
          What's wrong?

                          JAQUE
          We're losing him.

                          MAYA
          John? Don't go. Listen to us. You
          must listen. I have a message from
          Sadie.

                          JAQUE
          He's still there, barely. You must
          hurry, Maya.

                          MAYA
          She didn't love another. She loved
          you, John. It was you she loved. It
          was you!

(MAYA screams and goes limp in the chair. JAQUE checks his
instruments)

                          JAQUE
          He's gone. He's really gone.

                          FLO
          Really gone?

                                              (CONTINUED)

                    JAQUE
          He's no longer a restless spirit.
          He has moved on to the afterlife,
          that's what I mean by really gone.
          He now knows the truth and that has
          set him free.

                    REMMY
          But what about Sadie?

(JAQUE goes to MAYA and pats her on the hand)

                    JAQUE
          Maya? Can you hear me?

                    REMMY
          She looks so weak. Maybe we
          shouldn't push her.

                    JAQUE
          But we must know!

                    FLO
          We should let her rest first.

                    MAYA
               (Weakly)
          Jaque.

                    JAQUE
          I'm here, Maya. It's okay now.

                    MAYA
          Sadie is so upset. She didn't
          understand why John was dead. She
          didn't know he thought she was
          unfaithful. Oh, poor John. Poor
          Sadie. She was only trying to make
          him jealous so he'd pay more
          attention to her. The other man
          meant nothing to her. She just
          wanted John to think that so he'd
          want her more.

                    REMMY
          Oh, my gosh. That's so sad.

                    FLO
          But he's gone now...
          isn't he?

> JAQUE
> He's gone. I'm certain of it. My
> readings showed a vortex opening
> that allowed him to pass to the
> other side.

> FLO
> What about Sadie?

(JAQUE looks at MAYA who shakes her head no)

> JAQUE
> It's hard to say. I'm still getting
> some readings.

> MAYA
> She must still have unfinished
> business... it's with some other
> man. Al or Cal or Hal, I'm not
> sure.

> FLO
> We know an Al and a Cal.

> REMMY
> You don't think one of them had
> anything to do with their deaths?

> FLO
> I sure hope not.

> REMMY
> Is there anything we can do to help
> Sadie... uh... move along?

> MAYA
> Just speak to her when you sense
> her presence. Tell her you
> understand, let her know you're
> here for her. And maybe your
> kindness and understanding will
> help her move along too.

> JAQUE
> But I don't think you'll experience
> anything like that night again now
> that John has moved on.

> FLO
> Thank goodness.

(CONTINUED)

                    REMMY
          It would be wonderful if we could
          help Sadie and John move on
          together. They shouldn't be apart
          any longer.

(REMMY goes to MAYA)

                    REMMY (CONT.)
          Are you sure you're okay?

                    MAYA
          I could use something to drink.

                    FLO
          She said the magic words.

                    REMMY
          I think we might have a little
          something special in the car that
          will fix you right up.

(FLO and REMMY exit. JAQUE and MAYA drop their wacky
accents)

                    JAQUE
          We really shouldn't hang around any
          longer than we need to. The first
          rule of exorcism is get out fast
          before they ask too many questions.
          Now we're staying for drinks.

                    MAYA
          I have a feeling they have some
          other spirits if you know what I
          mean. That's a real treat.

                    JAQUE
          Just a quick sip and then we're
          leaving, got it?

                    MAYA
          Fine... fine... I'm just not in a
          hurry. Something really happened
          here tonight.

                    JAQUE
          What? Some of that was real?

                    MAYA
          Very.

                        JAQUE
          You haven't tapped in to anything
          in years.

                        MAYA
          I did this time. That was very
          strong. Sadie really wanted to be
          heard.

(PETE claps his hands in the darkness. JAQUE and MAYA are
startled)

                        PETE
          Brilliant performance. Must say I
          was convinced. You are as great as
          I remember, Maya.

                        MAYA
          Where did you come from?

                        PETE
          I didn't mean to startle you. You
          look like you just saw a ghost?

(PETE laughs at his joke)

                        JAQUE
          How long have you been in here...
          watching us?

                        PETE
          The whole time. That was quite a
          show.

                        MAYA
          That was no show. We do legitimate
          work.

                        JAQUE
          Yes, we are professionals.

                        PETE
          Professional con artists is what
          I'd say.

                        MAYA
          How dare you. This was quite real
          tonight.

                        PETE
          Now don't go get your knickers in a
          bunch. Your act is very
          convincing.

                                              (CONTINUED)

                         JAQUE
               This is no act.

                         PETE
               Yes, yes, so you claim. Between
               your little gadgets and the lady's
               performance, you have quite a thing
               going.

                         JAQUE
               I'll have you know that I have put
               years of research and study into
               what we do!

                         PETE
               Sure, sure. Can I see your gadget
               there?

                         JAQUE

               What?

                         PETE
               Can I see it?

                         JAQUE
               This is very sensitive equipment. I
               don't allow anyone to play with it.

(PETE is trying to get a look at it)

                         PETE
               Let me guess. When you say there's
               a ghost, you turn the flashing
               lights on and when the ghost starts
               to come or go you change how often
               it flashes I'd guess.

(JAQUE gets angry and clenches his fists)

                         JAQUE
               Now look here, buddy...

                         PETE
               Don't get violent. Remember, I'd
               admire your abilities to do this.
               Not anyone can do what you do.

                         JAQUE
               If you think we're frauds, then how
               did we know that stuff about the
               chair and ceiling?

                                              (CONTINUED)

                    PETE
          I'd guess that someone came in here
          and spied around. One of you
          interviewed people who come here a
          lot. I'm sure the owners have told
          the story a million times to a
          million people.

                    MAYA
          Why are we even talking to you?

                    JAQUE
          Maybe he was sent by Ghosts and
          Spirts, Inc. to discredit us.

                    PETE
          GAS? No, I checked them out and
          they're not nearly the pros you
          guys are.

                    JAQUE
          First right thing you've said all
          night.

                    PETE
          Let's cut to the chase. I want to
          hire you. I am willing to believe
          some it was real. Maya used to be
          the best before you stooped to your
          whole ghost buster for hire
          routine. And right now, I need the
          best... you think you can be the
          best again?

                    MAYA
          You think we're frauds and you want
          to hire us?

                    JAQUE
          Sorry, we don't work for people who
          doubt our abilities.

                    PETE
          I'll pay you five thousand dollars.

                    MAYA
          Five thousand?

                    PETE
          Each.

                    JAQUE
          Each?

                    MAYA
          How soon do you need us?

(She pulls out a small calendar and pencil)

                    PETE
          I'll expect you on Friday night at
          10 pm. We'll meet right here in
          this very building. I'll speak to
          the owners about it.

                    JAQUE
          Wait. We don't do return visits.

(MAYA grabs JAQUE roughly)

                    MAYA
          We will make an exception.

                    JAQUE
          So are you going to supply the
          ghost?

                    PETE
          She's already here. It's Sadie I'm
          interested in.

                    JAQUE
          Why her?

                    PETE
          She is connected to a murder and I
          want the killer brought to justice.

                    MAYA
          What can you tell us about this
          killer?

                    PETE
          That's why I need you, Maya.

                    JAQUE
          But with nothing to go on?

                    MAYA
          We can do it.

                    PETE
          That's what I thought. You were
          once the best. If anyone can handle
          this, you can.

                         MAYA
             We aim to please.

(JAQUE pulls MAYA aside)

                         JAQUE
             I have a bad feeling about this.
             Something tells me there's more
             here than meets the eye.

                         MAYA
             Hey, I'm the one who's supposed to
             have the funny feelings.

                         JAQUE
             So do you have any?

                         MAYA
             No, I don't. And even if I did, it
             wouldn't matter. He's offering us
             five thousand dollar each. We
             really need the money.

                         JAQUE
             But why is he offering so much?

                         MAYA
             There's probably a reward for
             catching the killer and he is going
             to split it with it. Maybe we can
             hold out for more money even. And
             besides... I feel a connection with
             Sadie. I want to help her. And
             we've done this sort of thing
             before and we can do it again.

                         JAQUE
             Or maybe this can be our last
             hurrah. Final proof that we're
             washed up. If we blow this one,
             that will be a sign to retire.
             Maybe I'm getting a little tired of
             playing ghost buster.

                         MAYA
             Retirement? Really?

                         JAQUE
             Look, tell the guy we'll do it. But
             keep in mind, if this goes sour on
             us, I'm done.

(MAYA goes to PETE)

                    MAYA
          We'll be here.

                    PETE
          Nifty. We'll be doing it as a
          little show. That's the
          cover. You'll be a performing
          psychic... we'll call the show...
          Seeing Beyond with Maya
          Fantasma. And we need an
          audience. Jaque... you'll be a
          plant in case Maya needs help...
          bring a friend too... you have a
          girlfriend?

                    JAQUE
          Yeah.

                    PETE
          Bring her.

                    JAQUE
          I don't know. She doesn't know
          anything about me and this ghost
          busting stuff.

                    PETE
          Please... we need as many people as
          we can get. I'll buy you dinner or
          something... at the Bee's Knees.

                    MAYA
          That's the hottest club in town.

                    PETE
          Fine, I'll bring her.

                    PETE
          Attaboy. I'll be looking forward
          to it.

                    MAYA
          As will we...

(MAYA pulls JAQUE aside again but this time PETE slips out)

                    MAYA (CONT.)
          This is so great. I just know this
          will go well. If we can put on a
          good show then we'll put GAS, Inc.
          out of business.

                         JAQUE
          This will either make or break us.
          That's for sure.

                         MAYA
          Oh, wait. Let me get his number...

                         JAQUE
          He's gone.

                         MAYA
          Weird.

                         JAQUE
          Spooky is what I say.

                         MAYA
          Come on. Let's get out of here. We
          have some planning to do.

                         JAQUE
          I still think something odd is
          going on. I can just feel it.

                         MAYA
          Look, I'm the only one who has
          funny feelings around here, okay?

(JAQUE and MAYA exit. Lights fade to black)

                    END OF SCENE

LOVING SOMEONE ELSE SONG

(Can be sung by JASMINE as SADIE or MADELINE as MAYA)

WHAT DO YOU MEAN BY LOVING SOMEONE ELSE (WHEN YOUR LOVE
BELONGS TO ME)

Sidney D. Mitchell / Archie Gottler, 1919

I've been worried all day long, 'Cause I know there's
something wrong, Tho' I've tried hard to smile, I have known
all the while, You're not as true as I've been to you. But
before I let you go, Here's one thing I'd like to know:

Every time I look at you, I don't know just what to do. I
can tell by your eyes are telling me lies, you'll go away
and leave me someday. But before we say farewell, There's a
thing you'll have to tell:

                                        (CONTINUED)

What do you mean by loving somebody else, When your love belongs to me? I found you when your kisses didn't have the taste, But now they've got the flavor, must they go to waste? What do you mean by teaching somebody else, All the things you learned from me? Just because I taught you how to roll your eyes, You don't have to run around and advertise, What do you mean by loving somebody else, When your love belongs to me?

CAUGHT

(MADELINE does a weird psychic meditation warm-up. BENDER studies her, trying to annoy her. PENNY and the others enter excited for another performance)

> PENNY
> You were all so great at our first performance.

> BRAD
> You were all like pros.

> HARM
> We just wanted to do a good job so we could get out of detention.

> PENNY
> But you were naturals. It was great.

> BRAD
> This show is so good.

> BRITNEY
> Speak for yourselves. I can't believe I'm stuck in this production with a bunch detention flunkies.

> HARM
> How'd you like a detention sandwich?

> BRITNEY
> How crude.

> HARM
> I'm going to kill her.

(JIMMY grabs a big pitcher of water and manages to get between HARM and BRITNEY. JIMMY dumps all the water on BRITNEY)

(CONTINUED)

                         JIMMY
          Ooops. Sorry about that Britney.

                         BRITNEY
          You did that on purpose. Now I
          have to do my makeup again. You...
          freaks!

(BRITNEY stomps out)

                         HARM
          Thanks, Jimmy. I would have killed
          her.

                         JIMMY
          Just wanted to save the show from
          disaster... and you...

                         HARM
          Why me?

                         JIMMY
          I don't want you stuck in detention
          forever.

                         HARM
          Why do you care?

                         JIMMY
          I just do.

                         HARM
          You doing it for me... or for
          yourself.

                         JIMMY
          What do you mean?

                         HARM
          If I killed Britney, maybe the show
          would be canceled tonight and you
          wouldn't get out of detention...

                         JIMMY
          No... I was thinking more about...
          you.

                         HARM
          You like me, don't you?

                         JIMMY
          Yeah.

                                          (CONTINUED)

                    HARM
          So why were you always pissing me
          off? Touching me and stuff?

                    JIMMY
          Because I liked you.

                    HARM
          You have to work on how you show
          it. Dunking Britney was good.

                    JIMMY
          And giving the principal a wedgie.

                    HARM
          You did that for me?

                    JIMMY
          Uh huh.

                    HARM
          That's kind of sweet.

                    JIMMY
          Really?

                    HARM
          Yeah, in a twisted sort of way...
          that's that way I like it...
          twisted.

                    JIMMY
          Twisted.

                    HARM
          I guess I'm glad you stopped me
          from killing Britney. I don't
          really want to ruin everyone's
          chance to get out of detention. I
          could care less about myself, but
          the rest of you I care about
          helping. I wouldn't want to
          disappoint all of you. I've never
          really looked at it like that
          before... that what I do might hurt
          others. I look out for number one,
          maybe I need to help out number two
          once in awhile.

                    JIMMY
          It feels good to be a part of
          something.

                    HARM
          So what you going to do with
          yourself when you are done with
          this play and out of detention?

                    JIMMY
          I was thinking of asking someone
          out on a date.

                    HARM
          Who would that be?

                    JIMMY
          Britney.

                    HARM
          Really? I think she'd say no.

                    JIMMY
          You actually.

                    HARM
          I kind of figured.

                    JIMMY
          You like bowling.

                    HARM
          No way... how did you know I liked
          bowling?

                    JIMMY
          And playing pool.

                    HARM
          You little stalker. You following
          me?

                    JIMMY
          Uh... uh...

                    HARM
          It's okay.

                    JIMMY
          Really?

                    HARM
          I've always wanted my own stalker.
          It's kind of cute.

(JIMMY blushes and can't speak)

                                          (CONTINUED)

                          HARM (CONT.)
                    Follow me, Jimmy. Time to get
                    ready for the show.

(JIMMY follows HARM happily off stage. GERTRUDE is setting
up again and PRINCIPAL appears. He sneaks up on her and
startles her)

                          PRINCIPAL
                    I found out, Gertrude. I know your
                    secret.

                          GERTRUDE
                    I don't know what you mean.

(PRINCIPAL hands her a letter. She opens it and her face
drops)

                          PRINCIPAL
                    It took some digging, but it looks
                    like you weren't completely honest
                    about your past... or your
                    degree... or much of anything. I
                    know our previous principal didn't
                    care much about anything besides
                    being "good with children" but
                    that's not how I run a
                    school. Please stop by my office
                    Monday morning with your letter of
                    resignation.

(GERTRUDE has tears in her eyes as the PRINCIPAL
exits. Lights fade to black)

                       END OF ACT I

ACT II SCENE 1 - SEEING BEYOND WITH MAYA FANTASMA

(The stage is simple with a chair and a backdrop. The
backdrop is a large display with writing on it saying Seeing
Beyond with Maya Fantasma. The lights show dimly on the
backdrop giving it an eerie appearance. JAQUE and VERA are
in the audience sitting near the DR corner of the stage. The
light suddenly gets very bright then a blackout. Spooky
music plays. There is a ghostly sounding ANNOUNCER. MAYA
enters in the darkness as the ANNOUNCER [PETE or JIMMY]
speaks)

                          ANNOUNCER
                    Welcome to Seeing Beyond with Maya
                    Fantasma. All you are about to see
                          (MORE)

                    ANNOUNCER (cont'd)
          is real. There are no tricks, no
          games, no acting involved. Maya
          Fantasma can really speak with the
          dead.

(Lights slowly come on. MAYA is in her seat, ready)

                    MAYA
          Hello, I'm Maya Fantasma. It's a
          pleasure to be here tonight. The
          spiritual activity here is intense.
          If there are times when I appear to
          be strained or overwhelmed please
          bare with me. Occasionally, the
          spirits are anxious to speak and
          their essences overpower me.
          Tonight will be one of those
          nights.
                    (She stands dramatically)
          Let's get started.

(She goes up to one audience member DL)

                    MAYA (CONT.)
          I feel drawn here. Something has
          brought me to you. I see someone
          about your height, though slightly
          shorter, wishing to talk to you. He
          has the same color hair as you.

(Waves her hand at audience member)

                    MAYA (CONT.)
          No, don't interrupt. Let me finish.
          I must not disrupt the connection.

(She closes her eyes a moment and touches the audience
members head)

                    MAYA (CONT.)
          He died from a blackening of the
          chest, could be a heart attack...
          could be a disease, it's hard to
          see.

(She backs away)

                    MAYA (CONT.)
          Wait. He wishes to speak. The dead
          speak in pictures, so I must
          interpret them for you. He says you
          always didn't get along but he
                    (MORE)

                                        (CONTINUED)

                         MAYA (CONT.) (cont'd)
                    still loves you. He says he is
                    sorry about the time he tipped over
                    the outhouse with you inside.

(Looks at audience member)

                         MAYA (CONT.)
                    Could this be your brother or
                    cousin or something?

(The audience member says no most likely)

                         MAYA (CONT.)
                    Maybe your father? Grandfather?
                    Uncle?

(No positive response)

                         MAYA (CONT.)
                    Well, this spirit is sorry anyway.

(She quickly moves on to another audience member DC. As she
heads to another, she sees SADIE near JAQUE and VERA. SADIE
points at VERA excitedly)

                         SADIE
                    It's her! It's actually her! This
                    is that woman! Did you bring her
                    here to me? What's she doing with
                    your friend? What is this all
                    about?!

(MAYA tries to ignore her and continues)

                         MAYA (CONT.)
                    I sense another presence. She
                    wishes to speak to you. She has
                    gray hair and is slightly shorter.
                    She died peacefully, but you were
                    worried she didn't. She...

(SADIE cries out in frustration. MAYA gives her a worried
look. JAQUE and VERA and rest of the actor audience don't
notice SADIE)

                         MAYA (CONT.)
                    She wants you to know she is near
                    you always. She watches over your
                    children as well.

                         SADIE
          Where does she come up with this
          stuff? The ghost here is yours
          truly... and I got a bone to pick
          with this one. Over here, Ms.
          Fantasma.

(MAYA gives SADIE a worried look again then moves on)

                         MAYA
          So many spirits trying to speak.

(SADIE jumps up excitedly and points to VERA)

                         SADIE
          Me next! Over here!

                         MAYA
          I sense another spirit.

(She goes L again)

                         SADIE
          No, this way. Come on.

                         MAYA
          Someone really wants to speak. I am
          being drawn...

                         SADIE
          Please. I'm dying to talk to her.

(MAYA speaks to an audience member)

                         MAYA
          You lost a pet recently?

                         SADIE
          A pet?! Oh come on. Let's channel
          some people.

(MAYA is on the verge of screaming at SADIE but controls
herself)

                         MAYA
          Within the last ten years you lost
          this family pet? Twenty maybe?
          Thirty?

(Keeps going until she gets a positive response. If not, go
to a person nearby and try again)

                    MAYA (CONT.)
          The pet wishes to let you know that
          she is okay and is waiting for you.

                    SADIE
          Maybe if I meow or bark or
          something...
          (Waves)
          Come on, over here.

(SADIE starts barking, meowing, oinking)

                    MAYA
          I must... I must, go.

                    SADIE
          What are you scared of? Come on. Do
          your thing.

                    MAYA
          Excuse me everyone. The spirits
          grow too strong. I must break and
          meditate.
          (Backs to exit)
          I will return in a moment.

                    SADIE
          She acts like she saw a ghost or
          something.

(MAYA exits. VERA stands)

                    VERA
          This is ridiculous. Let's go. She's
          obviously a fake.

                    JAQUE
          We still have time to kill before
          our reservation at the Bee's Knees.
          I think it's kind of funny.

                    VERA
          I want to go... now. Something
          weird is going on here.

                    SADIE
          You bet it is, dumb Dora.

(SADIE pokes VERA'S arm)

                    VERA
          Ah! What was that?

                          JAQUE
              Vera... take it easy. People are
              looking.

                          VERA
              But I felt something poke me.

                          JAQUE
              But there's nobody there.

                          VERA
              I felt it, I really did.

                          SADIE
              So you can feel me, huh? Can you
              hear me too?!

(SADIE pokes VERA again. VERA looks around but doesn't see
SADIE)

                          VERA
              It just happened again. And this
              time I thought I heard something.

                          JAQUE
              Maybe there really are ghosts here.

                          VERA
              There's no such thing.

(VERA says this more to convince herself than JAQUE)

                          SADIE
              Vera? Vera? Can you hear me?
              (Screams)
              Vera?!

                          VERA
              Did you hear that? Sounds like
              someone said my name. That's
              it. I'm leaving.

                          SADIE
              You're not getting out of here that
              easily.

(SADIE grabs VERA's purse from under her chair and hides it
under an audience member's chair)

                          VERA
              It's gone!

                    JAQUE
          What?

                    VERA
          My purse is gone.

                    JAQUE
          Maybe you left it in the bathroom.

(They exit. SADIE talks to audience as she retrieves purse
and places it in VERA's chair)

                    SADIE
          Have you ever looked all over the
          house and tired to find your purse
          or your car keys? Then suddenly you
          find them in plain sight. Now you
          know how this happens.

(MAYA peeks out, sees SADIE and disappears again)

                    SADIE (CONT.)
          That's it. I'm going to get her
          back out here.

(SADIE runs up and back to where MAYA is. SADIE follows MAYA
back out on stage)

                    MAYA
          I'm sorry, Sadie. It's been a long
          time since I've spoken to a spirit.
          It overwhelmed me.

                    SADIE
          Look, I need you because I heard
          you're the best. All the spirits
          tell me if anyone can help me you
          can.

(MAYA pulls SADIE aside and does a stage whisper)

                    MAYA
          I haven't seen a ghost in ten
          years. I've lost it.

                    SADIE
          Obviously you haven't. I'm here
          aren't I?

                    MAYA
          Yes, yes you are.

                                            (CONTINUED)

                         SADIE
          You channeled me the other night.
          Please do it again. You helped
          John, which I will be forever
          thankful to you for. But I have
          unfinished business too. I need
          you.

(Sees JAQUE and VERA returning)

                         SADIE (CONT.)
          Here she is. Let's do it.

                         VERA
          There's my purse. How did I miss
          that?

                         JAQUE
          Shush doll, I think the show
          started again.

                         VERA
          Let's go. This is
          terrible.   Terrible!

(VERA delivers the last word to the rest of the audience but
then MAYA blocks her exit)

                         MAYA
          Halt!

                         VERA
          Halt?

                         MAYA
          There is someone here who wishes to
          speak to you.

                         VERA
          Look, lady. I'm tired of the parlor
          tricks okay. We're leaving.

                         SADIE
          Tell Vera I know her little secret.

                         MAYA
          She knows your secret, Vera.

                         VERA
          She knows my name.

                        MAYA
          And this spirit knows your deepest,
          darkest secret.

                        SADIE
          Nice.

                        VERA
          I'm out of here.

                        SADIE
          Come on, Maya. Say my name. Don't
          let her go.

                        MAYA
          Her name is Sadie.

                        VERA
          No... not her.

                        JAQUE
          Who's Sadie?

                        VERA
          Nobody... not anymore.

                        SADIE
          Because of you!

                        MAYA
          What did you do, Vera?

                        VERA
          This isn't funny, Jaque. Please
          get me away from here.

                        JAQUE
          Who is Sadie? Why are you so
          afraid?

                        SADIE
          Because she knows how I died.

                        MAYA
          Vera knows how Sadie died.

                        JAQUE
          Do you, Vera?

                        VERA
          What's going on? Are you on their
          side too, Jaque? Why won't you
          help me?

(SADIE and MAYA are getting in sync. At first Maya speaks a
little after VERA but then starts speaking at the same time)

                    SADIE
          There is no help for you, Vera.

                    MAYA
          There is no help for you, Vera.

                    VERA
          Please... Jaque.

                    SADIE
          There is no escaping your crimes.

                    MAYA
          There is no escaping your crimes.

                    VERA
          Crimes? I didn't do anything
          wrong.

                    SADIE
          Liar!

                    MAYA
          Liar!

                    VERA
          Honest... it wasn't me. I saw it
          happen but it wasn't me. It was
          one of the big guys. One of the
          bosses. I swear.

                    SADIE
          I still see the blood on your
          hands.

                    MAYA
          I still see the blood on your
          hands.

(VERA looks at her hands fearfully)

                    SADIE
          The guilt in your eyes.

                    MAYA
          The guilt in your eyes.

                    SADIE
          The look of death in your eyes.

                    MAYA
          The look of death in your eyes.

                    VERA
          Please. Have mercy on me. I am a
          victim too. The bosses control our
          lives. Make us slaves.

                    SADIE
          Name the one who did this to me.

                    MAYA
          Name the one who did this to me.

                    VERA
          I can't... then they'll off me too.

(JAQUE gives MAYA a mad look)

                    JAQUE
          Please, Maya. That's enough. Not
          in front of all these people okay?

                    SADIE
          Please... make her confess. I must
          know the name of my killer.

                    MAYA
          That's enough, spirit.

                    SADIE
          No! Don't do this to me. I'm so
          close. You can't let it end this
          way.

                    MAYA
          It's too much... too much for me.

                    SADIE
          Don't let her get away with
          this. She's a trickster. She's
          even tricking your friend, Jaque.

                    MAYA
          What do you mean?

                    JAQUE
          What did she say?

                    SADIE
          Vera is cheating on him. She's
          about as loyal as Benedict Arnold.

                                        (CONTINUED)

                         MAYA
          Really? Are you sure?

                         JAQUE
          Tell me what she said.

                         MAYA
          She said that Vera is cheating on
          you.

                         JAQUE
          Is that true, Vera?

                         VERA
          What? No! What's the big
          idea? Spreading lies and rumors
          like that.

                         SADIE
          It's not a lie. It's true. She's a
          favorite of the Capones.

                         MAYA
          This is crazy.

                         VERA
          You're telling me. Let's go,
          Jaque. I'm pleading with you. How
          you watch her abuse me like this?
          Haven't you had enough?

                         JAQUE
          It sounds like there is a whole lot
          of funny business going on here.

                         SADIE
          You said it, fella.

                         JAQUE
          For some weird reason, the ghost
          knows you, Vera...

                         SADIE
          I do.

                         JAQUE
          In fact, she thinks you had
          something to do with her murder.

                         SADIE
          That's right.

                    JAQUE
And then she says you're cheating
on me.

                    SADIE
She is.

                    JAQUE
That leads me to believe one
thing...

                    SADIE
Let her have it.

                    JAQUE
That this is all a cover up...

                    SADIE
Really?

                    JAQUE
For the fact Maya is jealous of you
and me, Vera.

                    MAYA
What?!

                    SADIE
No!

                    VERA
That's right...

                    MAYA
Jaque! Have you gone mad?

                    SADIE
He's possessed... and poisoned.

                    VERA
That's the first smart thing I've
heard all night.

                    JAQUE
Are you just making this up,
Maya? Because you're jealous of
Vera? You've known me for a long
time... we're pretty close... but
not romantically close... are you
jealous because I have someone
besides you in my life? Do you
wish we had something instead so
you're making all this stuff up
about her?

                              MAYA
                    There's a ghost, right here,
                    telling me all this.

                              VERA
                    Or is there?

                              JAQUE
                    It's okay, Maya. You can tell me
                    the truth.

                              MAYA
                    I'm done... I can't do this
                    anymore. I want to use my talent to
                    bring comfort to people, not
                    torment them.
                    (Waves hand at SADIE)
                    Spirit, be gone!

(MAYA waves her hand at SADIE and SADIE is pushed back by
some invisible force)

                              SADIE
                    Wait! No! Vera is poisoning you
                    too.

                              MAYA
                    Away foul spirit.

                              SADIE
                    Foul? You're calling me foul?

                              MAYA
                    Let this torment stop.

                              SADIE
                    It's not me!

(SADIE rushes up and grabs MAYA)

                         MAYA AND SADIE
                    It's Vera!

(MAYA pulls away from SADIE)

                              VERA
                    Oh, please. Give it up already.
                    You're just a two bit fortune
                    teller who should never have taken
                    some acting classes.

                         JAQUE
          Yes, Maya. Stop this now.

                         MAYA
          Fine. I'll go then. I can see that
          I'm not wanted.

                         VERA
          Good. Don't let the portal to the
          spiritual world hit you on the butt
          on the way out.

                         MAYA
          And you can explain to the audience
          why they won't be getting the rest
          of their show tonight.

                         VERA
          What?

(MAYA stops and holds her hand to her forehead dramatically)

                         MAYA
          I predict everyone will demand a
          full refund and you'll have pay for
          it out of your own pocket.

(MAYA exits. VERA looks at audience)

                         VERA
          The audience wouldn't do that,
          would they?

(SADIE goes up to VERA and pokes her. VERA tries not to
react but is scared)

                         SADIE
          She's the reason I'm stuck. She's
          the reason I can't move on.

                         JAQUE
          I should really talk to Maya.

                         VERA
          Talk to her, Jaque and you're done
          talking to me. We're leaving this
          instant.

                         JAQUE
          But...

                              VERA
          Now!

(VERA drags JAQUE out)

                              SADIE
          This isn't over Vera. This is far
          from over.

                         END OF SCENE

THE SONG OF THE TEMPERANCE UNION

**Whole cast - taking turn with verses - with all of them
singing the chorus between each verse - all or part of this
song can be done.

We're coming, we're coming, our brave little band On the
right side of temp'rance we do take our stand. We don't use
tobacco, because we do think That the people who use it are
likely to drink

CHORUS: Away, away, with rum, by gum, Rum by gum, rum by gum
Away, away, with rum, by gum, The song of the Temperance
Union.

We never eat fruitcake because it has rum, And one little
slice puts a man on the bum. Oh, can you imagine the pitiful
plight Of a man eating fruitcake until he gets tight?

A man who eats fruitcake lives a terrible life. He's mean to
his children and beats on his wife. A man who eats fruitcake
dies a terrible death, With the odor of raisins and rum on
his breath!

We never eat cookies because they have yeast, And one little
bite turns a man to a beast. Oh, can you imagine the utter
disgrace Of a man in the gutter with crumbs on his face?

We never eat peaches because they ferment, And a peach will
ferment at the least little dent. Oh, can you imagine a
sight more obscene, Than a man getting tipsy on peaches and
cream!

Beware of plum pudding, the kind that they light. They
drench it in brandy so it will ignite. The thought is
revolting to temperate folk, For people go blotto inhaling
the smoke.

We never touch coffee; it makes our eyes gleam, At least when they add Irish whiskey and cream. Oh, can you imagine a fate more unkind Than sluggin' down coffee and going stone blind?

We never have backrubs because it's a crime, And we will oppose them in song and in rhyme. For an alcohol backrub is worse than straight gin When you think of the liquor absorbed through the skin.

Now if you go hiking and get sores on your feet, Don't use rubbing spirits as a means for to treat, 'Cause it seeps through the pores of your feet by osmosis, And you end up by having ten drunk little toesis.

We never eat cornflakes because they have malt, And we can't imagine a much greater fault. Oh, can you imagine a sight that's more droll Than a woman at breakfast slumped over her bowl!

ACT II SCENE 2 - STAY GOLDEN

                    BRITNEY
          Why aren't we doing the real
          history? Some of this stuff in the
          play is totally made up.

                    JIMMY
          Because tax evasion is boring. The
          real Al Capone was brought down by
          an accountant. Very anti-climatic.

                    BRITNEY
          Thank you, Encyclopedia Brown.

                    HARM
          Leave Jimmy alone, Bridiot.

                    BRITNEY
          Oh... am I insulting your
          boyfriend?

                    HARM
          How would you like my fist to be
          your boyfriend? He wants to smack
          you in the lips right now.

                    BRITNEY
          I'm telling!

                              HARM
          Not with a fat lip you're not.

                              PENNY
          Not now, Harm. We'll wait until
          the performances are done and then
          I promise I'll hold her down for
          you.

                              JIMMY
          We'll make a party of it. Cast
          party when the show is done and
          Britney can be the pinata.

                              HARM
          Fine.

                              BRITNEY
          Thanks... I think.

(GERTRUDE enters. She is clearly upset and has trouble
getting through the following, trying to seem super happy
but coming across as very sad)

                              GERTRUDE
          Wonderful to see you all here
          again. You've all been amazing and
          a real inspirations. I know I
          normally do a long speech before
          each performance... but you all
          don't need little old me to
          motivate you. You'll all doing
          terrific and have made me
          proud. Break a leg everyone.

(GERTRUDE exits quickly)

                              BRITNEY
          What's up with her?

                              PENNY
          She has a lot going on... things
          aren't easy for her right now.

                              HARM
          Principal Paine in the pants again?

                              PENNY
          Yeah.

                              JIMMY
          A man you love to hate.

                    JASMINE
          What's going on?

                    PENNY
          He's giving her a hard time about
          something... not sure what.

                    JASMINE
          I wish we could help her.

                    PENNY
          We can. By putting on the best
          performance possible.

                    BIFF
          Then that's what we do. Ready team?

                    JASMINE
          Ready!

(BIFF and JASMINE do some cheerleader moves and cheer. They
exit)

                    HARM
          Cheerleaders are so... cheerful.

                    JIMMY
          I used to hate them, but Biff and
          Jasmine ain't so bad.

                    HARM
          Yeah... makes me feel a little bad
          that I put sneezing powder in all
          the pompoms once before a game...
          just a little.

                    JIMMY
          No way... that was you?

                    HARM
          The one and only.

                    JIMMY
          You get more and more awesome every
          day.

                    HARM
          Stop being nice, okay? I don't
          like nice.

(But JIMMY can tell she does like it and is embarrassed)

                          JIMMY
            Right... I'll try to be insulting.
            Gotta work on my jerk
            material. I'll go hang out with
            Bender more.

                          HARM
            No... that's okay, Jimmy. Keep
            being you... stay golden, Pony Boy.

(HARM exits)

                          JIMMY
            Stay golden.

(He smiles and follows)

THE HYSTERICAL HISTORY OF THE GREAT DEPRESSION

(Spotlight on Bailiff [ideally played by a new actor but can
be played by BENDER or BIFF] rushes to PETE)

                          BAILIFF
            It was Capone.

                          PETE
            Which one?

                          BAILIFF
            Al.

                          PETE
            Tell me about it.

                          BAILIFF
            Capone ended up in front of Judge
            Rutherford...

                          PETE
            Oh great. Our most corrupt Judge
            facing off against our most
            notorious citizen.

                          BAILIFF
            It wasn't pretty.

(Lights come up and the stage is now transformed in to a
court room)

(Al CAPONE stands at the defendant's table smiling talking
and waving to the crowded courtroom [the "fans" of Al Capone

can either be on stage or in the audience as if the audience is a part of the courtroom]. RUTHERFORD, PERSON 1 and 2 can be played by BIFF, JASMINE, MADELINE or BENDER but ideally by new actors. A very nervous BAILIFF is trying to keep control)

                         BAILIFF
               Everyone. Sit down. Quiet! The
               judge will be here any moment.

                         CAPONE
               I appreciate you all coming here
               and showing your support today.

                         VERA
               We love you, Mr. Capone!

                         CAPONE
               I love you back, doll.

                         PERSON 1
               You're our hero, Capone!

                         CAPONE
               All of you are heroes to me. You
               all get out there every day and
               face the harsh world out there. No
               jobs, losing your homes, not sure
               where your next meal is coming
               from.

                         PERSON 2
               But you feed us. You give us jobs.

                         PERSON 1
               Who else does that?

                         VERA
               Why is he even here? This ain't
               right? They shouldn't have him on
               trial. They should have President
               Hoover on trial!

(People cheer at this. BAILIFF tries to get people to calm down)

                         PERSON 2
               Al Capone for President!

(People cheer more)

                         CAPONE
                "Vote early and often!"

(People laugh)

                         BAILIFF
                Settle down you! Or I'll run the
                lot of you in for disturbing the
                peace.

(People boo at BAILIFF who nervously backs away. A child
runs up to Capone and stands on a chair near him)

                         CHILD
                Thank you for the bicycle, Mr.
                Capone!

                         CAPONE
                You bet, kiddo.

                         VERA
                He buys kids bicycles, he feeds us
                with his soup kitchens, gets food
                to our kids in school, he gives us
                work. Set him free!

(People starts chanting)

                         CROWD
                Set him free! Set him free!

(Bailiff is really happy when he sees Judge Rutherford
appear)

                         BAILIFF
                Please rise for the honorable Judge
                Rutherford...

(People start booing. Judge, RUTHERFORD, gets up on bench
and gives the crowd a very evil stare. The booing dies
down. RUTHERFORD sits and CAPONE motions them to sit too)

                         RUTHERFORD
                I will clear this courtroom if
                there are any more outbursts from
                the mob gathered here.

                         CAPONE
                Don't worry, Judge. These good
                people won't disturb the peace... I
                assure you, they are no mob.

                                              (CONTINUED)

                         RUTHERFORD
             Well, you'd certainly know a mob if
             you saw one.

(Crowd starts to boo, RUTHERFORD bangs his gavel, BAILIFF
nervously reaches for his gun but CAPONE calms them down)

                         CAPONE
             Seems like you've been listening to
             rumors, Judge. I thought justice
             was blind.

                         RUTHERFORD
             Blind but not stupid, Mr.
             Capone. Sit down or I'll find you
             in contempt.

                         CAPONE
             Settle down, tiger.

                         RUTHERFORD
             You will refer to me at your honor!

                         CAPONE
             "Now I know why tigers eat their
             young."

(People laugh)

                         RUTHERFORD
             Bailiff!

                         CAPONE
             Now, now. "Don't you get the idea
             I'm one of those... radicals. Don't
             get the idea I'm knocking the
             American system." I'm all for
             justice.

                         RUTHERFORD
             Then you'll be pleased to hear I've
             replaced the jury with an entirely
             new group of people for your trial.
             It appears that the last jury was
             bribed.

                         CAPONE
             Bribed? How strange. By whom?

                         RUTHERFORD
             Don't play innocent with me. Your
             corruption is well known. You're a
             well-known leader of illegal
             enterprise...

                                        (CONTINUED)

                         CAPONE
          "I am like any other man. All I do
          is supply a demand."

                         RUTHERFORD
          You live like a King in a time when
          people are out of work and
          suffering.

                         CAPONE
          Judge, you live like a king and you
          ain't even earned it like me.

                         RUTHERFORD
          That's it! Bailiff!

(BAILIFF heads for CAPONE and reaches for a firearm but
court transcriptionist pulls a gun from her purse and holds
it at BAILIFF's head - if cast is limited, VERA can do this
instead)

                         CAPONE
          "You can get more with a nice word
          and a gun than you can with a nice
          word."

                         RUTHERFORD
          You're in contempt, Capone!

                         CAPONE
          I simply don't think you're the
          right man for this trial... your
          honor. Unless a corrupt man is
          more fit to judge corruption.

                         RUTHERFORD
          Bailiff!

                         BAILIFF
          Sorry, your honor. I'm a bit busy.

(Transcriptionist or VERA takes BAILIFF's gun and forces him
in to her seat)

                         CAPONE
          You say that I'm corrupt because of
          my success in a time of economic
          woe. But what about you... a
          servant of the people... how did
          you get so prosperous?

                                                        (CONTINUED)

                         RUTHERFORD
              I'm not on trial here, Capone.

                         CAPONE
              Maybe you should be.

(People cheer. PERSON 1 and 2 grab Rutherford. CAPONE
takes Judge's spot on the bench)

                         RUTHERFORD
              Unhand me! Get down from there!

                         CAPONE
              Order in the court.

(People laugh)

                         CAPONE (CONT.)
              So who should be on trial here... a
              man who helps the people or a man
              who uses abuses his honorable
              position for person gain?

                         RUTHERFORD
              I don't have to listen to this.

                         CAPONE
              But you do. Sit down.

(PERSON 1 and 2 force RUTHERFORD in to defendant's chair)

                         CAPONE (CONT.)
              Now I may have two homes, but you
              have five, your honor. I have a
              Cadillac... you have two. I have a
              yacht... you have two. While I'm
              completely sober at work...

(CAPONE pulls out a flask from the bench.)

                         CAPONE (CONT.)
              You appear to get quite drunk.

(People react strongly to CAPONE pulling out the flask)

                         RUTHERFORD
              You planted that there. That's not
              mine.

                         CAPONE
              Your honor... how did you come by
              alcoholic beverages during
              Prohibition?

                         RUTHERFORD
              It's not mine!

                         CAPONE
              What's this engraving on the
              flask? Initials? JFR?

                         VERA
              Joseph Franklin Rutherford!

                         RUTHERFORD
              No, JFR could mean anything.

                         CAPONE
              Justice For Rich? Just For
              Rutherford? Jump For Riches?

(People laugh)

                         CAPONE (CONT.)
              All in favor of the honorable Judge
              Rutherford going to jail instead
              citizen Capone say ay!

                         PEOPLE
              Ay!

                         CAPONE
              Take him away!

(PERSON 1 and 2 are joined by others and drag off
RUTHERFORD and BAILIFF. VERA goes up to CAPONE and sits by
him. He gives her the flask and she takes a drink)

                         CAPONE (CONT.)
              "This American system of ours, call
              it Americanism, call it capitalism,
              call it what you will, gives each
              and every one of us a great
              opportunity if we only seize it
              with both hands..."

(CAPONE grabs VERA by the shoulders)

                         CAPONE (CONT.)
              "...and make the most of it"

(CAPONE tries to kiss VERA. She squeals and runs. CAPONE
chases her)

                         CAPONE (CONT.)
              Life! Liberty! and the Pursuit of
              Happiness!

END OF SCENE

ACT II SCENE 3 GERTY GONE

(Everyone is rushing around getting ready for another
performance. MADELINE does her usual weird psychic
meditation warm-up. BENDER studies her once again trying to
annoy her. PRINCIPAL walks in observing. HARM notices and
gets the others attention)

                    PRINCIPAL
          Good evening everyone.

                    HARM
          What are you doing here?

                    PRINCIPAL
          I'm here every night.

                    HARM
          This is backstage, bub. Actors and
          directors only.

                    PRINCIPAL
          That's the problem. No director.

                    PENNY
          What do you mean?

                    PRINCIPAL
          I'm afraid your director, Mrs.
          Fenstermacher, will not be making
          it tonight.

                    PENNY
          What happened to her?

                    PRINCIPAL
          She has resigned.

                    BRAD
          What? No!

                    BIFF
          Resigned? What are you talking
          about?

                    PRINCIPAL
          It turns out she was telling quite
          a lie. She actually was not a
          teacher. She had a fake degree
                    (MORE)

                                         (CONTINUED)

                    PRINCIPAL (cont'd)
          from a fake school, Shaftesbury
          University which is not a real
          institution of learning.

                    PENNY
          But she was the best teacher I ever
          had.

                    PRINCIPAL
          Really? Actually she was a terrible
          influence on you, Penny. She
          turned you in to a criminal.

                    PENNY
          I didn't think what you were doing
          to her was right. I had to do
          something.

                    PRINCIPAL
          Two wrongs do not make a right.

                    PENNY
          You talk like you're good, but
          you're horrible. How dare you do
          this to her. You're a terrible
          person.

                    PRINCIPAL
          That's enough, Penny. That will
          get you plenty more detention. And
          not this fake made up detention
          that was more of a reward than a
          punishment for you. In fact, that
          goes for the rest of you. None of
          you get any time off from detention
          for this recreational activity.

(All react with anger)

                    HARM
          You can't do that.

                    BIFF
          That's bogus, dude. We were made a
          promise.

                    BENDER
          I'm out of here.

(JIMMY and BRAD stop BENDER)

                    PRINCIPAL
          I'd understand if you all just
          walked out of here now. I'll go
          cancel the performance and let the
          audience know they can go home.

                    BIFF
          No, we're going to do the show.

                    JASMINE
          That's right. We'll do it for Mrs.
          Fenstermacher. What do you say
          everyone?

                    BRAD
          I'm in.

                    JIMMY
          Me too.

                    MADELINE
          I'll do it.

                    BENDER
          Oh, why not. I like playing a
          gangster.

(Does machine gun sounds at PRINCIPAL)

                    PRINCIPAL
          Fine. One more performance. But
          this is closing night. And all of
          you can report to detention on
          Monday.

(PRINCIPAL exits)

                    PENNY
          Thank you everyone. This means so
          much to me and I know Mrs.
          Fenstermacher would be proud of all
          of you.

                    HARM
          I can't believe this. I wanna
          string up that creep. I don't know
          if I can do this.

                    JIMMY
          Please, Harm. I have a plan.

                      HARM
         A plan?

                      JIMMY
         On how we can get back at Principal
         Paine.

                      HARM
         I'm listening.

                      JIMMY
         Okay, everyone. This is what we'll
         do.

LITTLE CRUMBS OF HAPPINESS

(Song and Lyrics by J. Keirn Brennan and Ernest R. Ball.
Sung by JASMINE as SADIE or PENNY as REMMY or MADELINE AS
MAYA)

First Verse

You could not give me all your love, Although I know you
tried; But what you gave made me your slave, And I was
satisfied.

Second Verse

What food you brought for loving though, Within your tender
eyes; In your one kiss, one taste of bliss, I found life's
greatest prize.

Chorus

Little crumbs of happiness That fell like golden grain,
Filled my hungry, homesick heart And stilled that lonesome
pain. Little drops of tenderness That made me love you so;
Little crumbs of happiness You gave me long ago.

THE CREEPY CORPSE OF CAL CAPONE

****OPTIONAL SCENE A********

(Various people are gathered in a club talking, drinking,
and enjoying themselves. Everyone is dressed casually except
for REMMY who wears a nice, white dress. The center of
attention is FLO and SAM, who are arm wrestling. SAM is
straining. FLO is relaxed)

                                                    (CONTINUED)

                         SAM
          You give up yet?

                         FLO
          What's the matter, Sam? Tired.

                         SAM
          No way.

                         JAQUE
          Any more bets? Flo's looking tired.

(FLO starts to weaken)

                         SAM
          I've got you now.

                         SALLY
          Twenty more dollars on Sam!

                         FLO
          How much we got, Jaque?

                         JAQUE
          That makes two hundred dollars for
          the winner.

                         FLO
          That's enough. Come to mommy!

(FLO kisses the money)

                         SAM
          You cheated us!

                         SALLY
          That ain't fair. We want our money
          back.

                         FLO
          A bet's a bet.

(SAM pulls out a gun. REMMY comes out during this, sees gun
and grabs a metal skillet)

                         SAM
          And a gun's a gun.

(REMMY hits SAM over the head and he falls)

                         REMMY
          You know the rules. No guns.

                                               (CONTINUED)

(REMMY picks the gun up like a dirty diaper and throws it away. SALLY runs over to SAM and pats his face to try and wake him up)

> SALLY
> Sam? Sam? Speak to me.

> SAM
> Wow, what a headche.

> SALLY
> Oh, Sam. I'm so glad you're okay.

> SAM
> Sure, I'm okay... uh... what did you say your name was?

> SALLY
> Oh, Sam. You're gonna make me cry.

(SALLY runs out in tears)

> SAM
> What happened?

> FLO
> Well, you see. Jaque was returning your money and you dropped it on the floor under the table. You were reaching for your money and then you hit your head. That's when this guy grabbed your money and ran out the door.

> SAM
> What?

> FLO
> You better go get it. He's got a big head start.

> SAM
> I'll kill him!

(SAM runs out angrily)

> JAQUE
> Nice story.

> FLO
> Thanks.

*******END OPTIONAL SCENE A**************

(CONTINUED)

(There's a knock at the door: shave and a haircut)

                    REMMY
          It's the secret knock. Open the
          door.

(JAQUE opens the door and SIMON walks in)

                    JAQUE
          Who are you?

(Everyone looks nervously at SIMON)

                    SIMON
          Simon. Sim Simon.

                    REMMY
          Can I help you?

                    SIMON
          The sign outside said, "Pete's
          Pickled Pig Toes." Is this where I
          can get some pickled pig toes?

                    REMMY
          Well, not exactly.

                    SIMON
          You're out of business?

                    REMMY
          Well...

                    SIMON
          You're not....

                    REMMY
          Ummm...

                    SIMON
          This isn't...

                    REMMY
          Uh...

                    SIMON
          An illegal operation?

                    REMMY
          Please, sir... this isn't what it
          looks like.

                         SIMON
          As a loyal citizen of this
          wonderful nation I must...

(PETE pulls out a gun and points it at SIMON)

                         SIMON (CONT.)
          ...say that I didn't see a thing.

                         PETE
          Good choice.

(PETE guides SIMON out the door)

                         FLO
          Nice to have Pete as a bouncer.

(VERA pulls FLO aside)

                         VERA
          So what's the deal with Pete?

                         FLO
          What do you mean?

                         VERA
          I swear I've seen him before...
          right along Elliot Ness... one of
          them Untouchables.

                         FLO
          He's untouchable alright. If only
          he were unsmellable too. That guy
          stinks.

                         VERA
          So is he?

                         FLO
          What?

                         VERA
          You know... the fuzz... a copper...
          one of them guys that just took
          down Al Capone.

                         FLO
          Don't mention Al around here right
          now. His younger brother, Cal,
          owns this club and he's pretty sore
          about his brother getting nabbed.

                                      (CONTINUED)

                    VERA
         Can you believe it... Al Capone...
         thrown in jail for cheating on his
         taxes.

                    FLO
         Shhh... nix the Al talk, toots.

                    VERA
         So tell me more this Pete then.

                    FLO
         Pete doesn't like to talk about his
         past either... and his fall from
         grace.

                    VERA
         Fall from grace?

                    FLO
         They say he got in fight with Eliot
         Ness himself.

                    VERA
         Really... the leader of the
         Untouchables?

                    FLO
         A fist fight... on top of a
         skyscraper... he nearly knocked ol'
         Ness off with a nasty left hook.

                    VERA
         What were they fighting over?

                    FLO
         A woman.

                    VERA
         Of course. Then what happened?

                    FLO
         Then Pete ends up here... a bouncer
         at a speakeasy... disgraced.

                    VERA
         Wow.

                    FLO
         You said it, toots.

(BETH goes to gossip about PETE with some others. REMMY
goes to FLO)

                                              (CONTINUED)

                          REMMY
          Nice cover story for Pete.

                          FLO
          Had to come up with something. She
          was getting nosey.

                          REMMY
          Spying for Cal?

                          FLO
          Dunno. Probably. Better safe than
          sorry.

(Knock at the door - shave and a haircut)

                          JAQUE
          It's the secret knock. I'll get it.

*** OPTIONAL SCENE B IF HAVE ENOUGH ACTORS FOR COP, KID AND
DRUNK**

(A KID appears at the door. This can be the same kid from
the courtroom scene)

                          KID
          You got any pickled pigs toes?

(JAQUE slams the door on the KID)

                          JAQUE
          You gotta change that password,
          Remmy.

                          FLO
          So what's on the schedule tonight?

                          BETH
          Yea, we want some entertainment!

                          REMMY
          I was hoping you wouldn't ask.

                          FLO
          Where's the band?

                          JAQUE
          Where's the singer?

(An old DRUNK gets up and goes center)

                                        (CONTINUED)

                              DRUNK
                    I'm gonna sing for you now... one
                    of my favorite songs...

                              FLO
                    This should be good.

                              DRUNK
                    For your information, I was a
                    talented actor in my day. Did some
                    real serious theatre at one time.

                              BETH
                    I'll bet you really knocked 'em
                    dead.

                              FLO
                    Yeah, with his breath.

                              DRUNK
                    Go ahead and laugh. Once you hear
                    me sing you'll be
                    sorry. Maestro? A one, a two,
                    a....

(DRUNK passes out on the floor. Everyone applauds)

                              JAQUE
                    Beautiful! Bravo!

                              FLO
                    Stunning performance.

                              BETH
                    Encore! Encore!

(PETE drags off the drunk)

                              REMMY
                    Anyone else want to give it a try?

                              JAQUE
                    No one can top that.

(Knock at door)

                              JAQUE
                    That's not the secret knock.

                              REMMY
                    Quick everyone. To your places.

(Everyone rushes around and hides liquor and changes gambling for checkers, etc. Jars of pickles are set out. More knocking)

                         JAQUE
          That sounds like a cop.

                         REMMY
          Oh, my. Oh, my. Where's Pete?

                         JAQUE
          Ready?

                         REMMY
          Let 'em in.

(JAQUE lets in the COP. He enters with the DRUNK. He draws his gun and the DRUNK falls to the floor)

                         COP
          Surprise! Police raid!

                         JAQUE
          Come on in, officer.

                         REMMY
          Care for any pickled pig toes?

                         COP
          Sorry, ma'am. I thought this was an
          illegal booze operation.

                         REMMY
          As you can see, this is a reputable
          joint.

                         COP
          I'm sure I smelled some alcohol on
          this drunk I just found outside of
          here.

                         REMMY
          It must be the stuff we pickle
          with. People often make that
          mistake.

(The COP points to the DRUNK)

                         COP
          So what's with him?

                         REMMY
          Oh, he's in charge of... tasting
          the pickling juice... to make sure
          it's the right mixture.

                         COP
          You sure that's safe?

                         REMMY
          He isn't dead is he?

(COP nudges DRUNK with his foot)

                         COP
          I don't know. I can't tell.

                         REMMY
          Trust me, he's fine.

(COP looks at a jar of pickles)

                         COP
          These look like pickles.

                         REMMY
          That's what happens when you pickle
          pigs' feet. They turn out just
          like pickles.

                         COP
          Well, what do you know?

                         REMMY
          Amazing, isn't it?

(REMMY guides the COP toward the door)

                         REMMY (CONT.)
          I suppose you'll want to be going.

                         COP
          I do have to go. Sorry to disturb
          you all.

                         REMMY
          Don't mention it. Bye.

(REMMY pushes him out the door)

                         REMMY (CONT.)
          That was close.

(Everyone changes the place back as before. REMMY sighs and
then there is another knock at the door)

                                              (CONTINUED)

                              REMMY (CONT.)
                    Here we go again.

(Everyone starts changing back again. COP opens door)

                              COP
                    I just wanted to say...

(REMMY tries to close door on him. Everyone is frantic and
confused)

                              REMMY
                    What's that?

                              COP
                    If you every need anything, give me
                    a call.

                              REMMY
                    Okay, thank you.

(REMMY pushes him out and shuts the door)

                              REMMY (CONT.)
                    That was way too close.

(They start to change back and then there's another knock)

                              REMMY (CONT.)
                    I'm going to kill him.

(REMMY grabs her frying pan)

                              JAQUE
                    No, Remmy!

(REMMY opens the door and is about the swing her frying pan)

                              REMMY
                    I've had it with you!

(CAL enters with PETE. She clobbers PETE by accident)

                              CAL
                    That's a fine how do you do.

                              REMMY
                    Pete! I'm so sorry.

********END OF OPTIONAL SCENE B********

                         VERA
               Back about your business. It's the
               Boss.

(They greet him warmly - but it's fake)

                         ALL
               Cal!

                         CAL
               Hello, everyone. This kind greeting
               is all very touching. But I'm
               afraid I'm closing you down.

(They all turn angry and show their true feelings for him)

                         ALL
               What?!

                         REMMY
               You can't mean it.

                         CAL
               You just ain't making enough money,
               Ms. Remmington. And you have cops
               hanging around outside your
               door. This ain't no way to run a
               business.

                         REMMY
               I don't know what you're talking
               about.

                         VERA
               He has ways of knowing what's going
               on around her.

(VERA goes and cuddles up to CAL. JAQUE is upset)

                         JAQUE
               What are you doing, Vera?

                         VERA
               You're such a fool. You really
               think I'm your loyal little
               girlfriend? Sure, we had a few
               laughs but need a man with a little
               more... substance.

                         FLO
               She means money.

                        VERA
          And power.

                        JAQUE
          So it's true... you're a two faced
          liar.

                        CAL
          I'd call her a talented double
          agent.

                        REMMY
          This isn't fair. You can't close
          the club.

                        FLO
          Who needs you. We can make our own
          club.

(PETE starts to get up and CAL grabs REMMY's frying pan)

                        CAL
          If you don't use my clubs... you
          don't use any club.

(CAL hits PETE with the frying pan and he passes out again.
VERA picks up some paper and he cuts out a paper person
during the following)

                        CAL (CONT.)
          And you know what happens to people
          who walk into someone else's club.
          They don't walk anymore.

(VERA rips the legs off of the paper person. People gasp in
reply)

                        REMMY
          Okay, Cal. We get the point.

                        FLO
          You don't need this guy, Remmy. You
          can get along just fine without
          him.

(CAL takes out a document)

                        CAL
          Actually she can't.

                        FLO
          What's that?

                         CAL
          Her contract.

                         REMMY
          Contract with the devil.

                         CAL
          She was thrown out in the street.
          Desperate and penniless, she came
          to me. I agreed to help on one
          condition: she had to sign this.

                         FLO
          You can't hold her to that. It's
          just a piece of paper.

                         CAL
          I certainly can... because Remmy is
          a woman of honor.

                         REMMY
          I gave my word.

                         CAL
          And she signed in blood.

                         FLO
          Ew... really?

                         CAL
          But you've failed me, Remmy. You've
          broken section 1 of our contract.
          Now it's on to section 2.

                         REMMY
          Oh, no. Not section 2. Anything but
          section 2.

                         FLO
          What's section 2?

                         REMMY
          It's too horrible. I can't even
          say it. It's a fate worse than
          death.

(CAL reads the document)

                         CAL
          Section 2 reads: "Anyone who fails
          to do business for Cal Capone will
          be condemned to mixing whiskey at
          his underground factory."

                                        (CONTINUED)

                    FLO
          That can't be legal.

                    CAL
          Legal, smeegle. We left legal
          outside the door.

                    REMMY
          I know I'm not making the kind of
          money you're used to but the prices
          you're charging...

                    CAL
          The prices are fine.

                    REMMY
          Give me one more month...

                    CAL
          I gave you one more month...

                    REMMY
          I'll do anything to keep this club
          open.

                    CAL
          Anything?

                    REMMY
          Well...

                    FLO
          Think about that one carefully,
          Remmy.

                    CAL
          Stay out of this.

                    REMMY
          Anything.

                    CAL
          Anything?

                    REMMY
          Anything!

(CAL does an evil laugh)

                    CAL
          Then we will marry at midnight.

                         REMMY
          Marry?

                         ALL
          Marry?!

                         CAL
          Married. M-A-R-Y-D. Married.

                         REMMY
          Oh, no.

                         CAL
          Oh, yes.

                         REMMY
          Oh, my.

                         CAL
          Oh, boy. See you tonight. Wear
          something white.

(VERA blows JAQUE a kiss)

                         VERA
          See ya.

(CAL starts to exit with VERA. PETE is up again and blocking
the way)

                         CAL
          Move it, creep.

(CAL tries to push past PETE but he blocks the way)

                         PETE
          You're going to be sorry,
          Cal. You're going to be real sorry
          you're doing this to Remmy.

                         CAL
          Is that a threat?

                         PETE
          Nope, just a prediction.

                         CAL
          Oh, you a psychic?

                         PETE
          Naw... this seems like a sure
          thing.

(VERA hits PETE with the frying pan and he passes out)

                                              (CONTINUED)

                              CAL
                  Did you see that one coming too?

(CAL and VERA laugh and exit. REMMY runs to PETE's side to
see if he is okay)

                              JAQUE
                  I can't believe this.

                              FLO
                  Yeah... Remmy married to
                  Cal. That's is a fate worse than
                  death.

                              JAQUE
                  I'm talking about, Vera. How could
                  she do this to me?

                              FLO
                  That seems like the least of our
                  worries right now. You're better
                  off without her.

                              JAQUE
                  I feel terrible... not that she was
                  a prize but think of how I treated
                  Maya. Maya was such a good friend
                  and I treated her so badly when she
                  told me her suspicions about Vera.
                  I need to to talk to Maya... I need
                  to apologize. I feel like such a
                  heel.

(JAQUE leaves and FLO goes to REMMY)

                              FLO
                  What are you thinking, Remmy?! You
                  can't marry Cal.

(REMMY tries to wake up PETE)

                              REMMY
                  It's all part of the plan. Now if
                  Pete would wake up, we could find
                  out what that plan is.

                              PETE
                  Remmy? Is that you, my love?

                              FLO
                  My love?

                    REMMY
          Shh... Pete. Everyone's listening.

                    PETE
          Oh, no. I'm sorry... I didn't mean
          to...

                    REMMY
          It's okay. We couldn't keep it a
          secret forever.

                    FLO
          Wait... what? You two?

                    REMMY
          We found love in the middle of my
          worst nightmare.

(REMMY and PETE join hands)

                    PETE
          I hope I can turn this nightmare in
          to your most wonderful dream,
          Remmy. At first, I was undercover,
          trying to find dirt on the
          Capones. But Remmy touched my
          heart and I knew I had to help
          her... help her get free of their
          evil grip. She was an innocent
          victim that I couldn't see
          destroyed by them. The stronger my
          love grew for her, the more
          determined I became to take down
          the Capones.

                    REMMY
          Oh, Pete. What can we do? Do you
          think we can really get Cal now?

                    PETE
          For starters, we now have this.

(PETE pulls out Cal's contract)

                    REMMY
          My contract!

                    FLO
          How did you get that?

                    PETE
          I lifted it from him when I ran in
          to him as he was leaving.

                         FLO
          Way to go!

                         REMMY
          You've saved me.

                         PETE
          But we still have to put him
          away... so he never bothers you...
          or anyone... again.

                         FLO
          How are we going to do that?

                         PETE
          We're going to have a wedding...
          with a surprise guest. Cal has
          some skeletons in his closet. Now
          we need to invite one of them to
          his wedding. So here's the plan...

(They huddle as the lights fade to black)

CREEPY CORPSE SCENE 2

(MAYA enters. She still is dressed as a psychic but perhaps
is done up more attractively in order to get Jaque's
attention)

                         JAQUE
          I'm so glad you came.

                         MAYA
          I am here to help Remmy and Pete
          deal with Cal Capone.

                         JAQUE
          I really wanted to talk to you...

                         MAYA
          We need to stay focused. We haven't
          much time.

                         JAQUE
          I just need to talk... just for a
          minute.

                         MAYA
          I must have complete silence in
          order to commune with the spirits.

(SADIE shows up immediately)

                    SADIE
          I'm here... let's here what cutie
          here has to say.

                    MAYA
          Cutie?

                    JAQUE
          What?

                    MAYA
          Nothing.

                    SADIE
          He is very cute. If I were alive
          I'd snatch him right up.

                    MAYA
          This is serious. We have a job to
          do here.

                    JAQUE
          I know, but... I don't think I can
          wait.

                    SADIE
          Don't make sweetie wait. Look at
          those puppy dog eyes. He's hurting
          inside.

                    MAYA
          I don't care.

                    JAQUE
          Look. I know I hurt you. But I
          didn't know there were feelings
          there to hurt.

                    MAYA
          Everyone has feelings, Jaque.

                    SADIE
          You sure don't act like it
          sometimes.

                    MAYA
          What is that supposed to mean?

                    JAQUE
          Uh... is someone else here, Maya?

                         MAYA
              Yes, our ghost has arrived. Let's
              get to work.

                         SADIE
              I'm not doing anything until you
              listen to sweetie pie. I want to
              know what he has to say. Maybe I
              should knock him off and keep him
              for myself?

                         MAYA
              Don't you dare.

                         JAQUE
              What is she saying?

(SADIE whispers loudly in his ear)

                         SADIE
              That you're a cutie pie.

(JAQUE's ear is tickled by this and he touches it with a
chuckle)

                         MAYA
              Fine. Hurry up and say your peace.
              We have work to do but obviously
              neither one of you will do anything
              until we talk.

                         JAQUE
              Thank you, Sadie.

(SADIE whispers in JAQUE's other ear)

                         SADIE
              You're welcome, sweetums.

(JAQUE is tickled again)

                         MAYA
              Stop that.

                         SADIE
              You're no fun.

                         JAQUE
              So... Maya... I need to tell you
              how sorry I am... sorry that I
              didn't believe you about Vera...
              sorry I treated you the way I
              did... but...

                                            (CONTINUED)

                    MAYA
          There is always a but.

                    JAQUE
          Well... I didn't know you had
          feelings for me.

                    MAYA
          I guess I didn't either. But when I
          saw how evil Vera was and how
          deeply she was getting her claws in
          to you... something happened...
          these feelings welled up inside me
          that I've never had before.

                    SADIE
          Jealousy... envy... love...

                    MAYA
          Yeah...

                    JAQUE
          You are the most amazing person
          I've even know, Maya. I never
          thought in a million years you'd be
          interested in me.

                    MAYA
          Why not?

                    JAQUE
          You were like a celebrity to me. I
          admired your work and was a fan...
          when you took me on as an
          assistant, I was thrilled to be
          working with you. I nearly
          worshiped you, but never considered
          you'd have any feelings for me in
          return.

                    SADIE
          She doesn't seem to have many
          feelings at all.

                    MAYA
          Stay out of this, Sadie.

                    SADIE
          I'm just saying you hide your
          feelings, Maya.

                    MAYA
          Do I hide my feelings?

                    JAQUE
          You're all business, all the time.

                    MAYA
          I guess you're right. I was more
          focused on my work... than
          anything.

                    JAQUE
          Relationships were not on your
          mind.

                    MAYA
          No.

                    JAQUE
          Are they now?

                    SADIE
          Yes!

(MAYA glares at SADIE)

                    SADIE (CONT.)
          Sorry... buttoning my lips.

                    MAYA
          I do care deeply for you, Jaque...
          I enjoyed being with you more than
          anyone before. We worked so well
          together... it's like you knew what
          I needed before I did.

                    JAQUE
          I guess I'm a little psychic too.

                    MAYA
          It's a nice feeling to have someone
          at your side that doesn't have to
          be told everything.

                    JAQUE
          So I'm a good work partner.

                    MAYA
          You're much more than that. You
          were a wonderful friend too.

                          SADIE
           Come on, Maya.

(MAYA glares at SADIE who buttons her lip again)

                          MAYA
           But I started feeling so much more.

                          JAQUE
           Me too. Especially when I knew I
           hurt you.

                          MAYA
           It did hurt... very badly that you
           believed Vera over me. I couldn't
           believe you didn't trust me after
           all we'd been through together.

                          JAQUE
           I'm so sorry, Maya. You're right. I
           treated you so poorly. I understand
           why you are upset at me. But I had
           to try and talk to you and tell
           you... that I have feelings for you
           too. Strong feelings. Feelings I
           can't ignore any more.

(SADIE gets excited)

                          SADIE
           Kiss him, kiss him, kiss him!

(MAYA glares at SADIE)

                          MAYA
           Tell you what... when this is all
           over, let's go something...
           private... to talk. Just the two
           of us.

                          JAQUE
           Sounds good.

                          MAYA
           Can we get to work now, Sadie?

                          SADIE
           Fine. What's the plan to get, Cal
           Capone?

                          MAYA
           Follow me.

(Lights fade to black as Maya leads Sadie and Jaque off)

CREEPY CORPSE SCENE 3

(Lights come up slightly on VERA entering a darkened club)

                         VERA
          Where is everybody? The boss
          wanted me to make sure everything
          was A-okay, but there ain't nothing
          here period. Kind of fishy if you
          ask me.

(MAYA appears from behind her in the dark and hits her over
the head with a frying pan. VERA passes out and MAYA drags
her off - FLO can help if needed. After a moment, CAL
enters. If extra actors are available to play bodyguards,
CAL can tell them to "wait outside and make sure nobody
interrupts the festivities")

                         CAL
          Hello? Where is my little muffin?
          Is she ready for the big day?

(REMMY comes in sobbing wearing black)

                         REMMY
          I... I... I'm ready.

                         CAL
          Good. Hey, nice dress.

                         REMMY
          Is that all you can say? This is
          the worst day of my life and all
          you can say is "nice dress."

                         CAL
          Okay, uh... you're hair looks good
          too.

                         REMMY
          This is the worst day of my life.

                         CAL
          Aw... you say the sweetest
          things. Where is that priest?

(JAQUE and FLO enter)

                         REMMY
          At least my friends are here.

                                        (CONTINUED)

>   JAQUE
> We couldn't skip out on you, Remmy.

>   FLO
> We knew you could use some backup.

>   REMMY
> You can say that again.

>   FLO
> We knew you could...

>   CAL
> Shut up! All of yous! I want this
> to be over with as soon as
> possible.

(Everyone stands nervously in silence a moment)

>   JAQUE
> Did you get a cake?

>   CAL
> I said quiet!

(They are quiet again for a few moments)

>   FLO
> What about a bouquet?

(CAL pulls out a gun)

>   CAL
> I said shut up! Next person who
> talks, gets it!

(PETE enters in disguise as the priest)

>   PETE (AS PRIEST)
> Hello, my children.

(CAL points gun at him)

>   PETE (CONT.)
> Sorry I'm late.

>   CAL
> Oh, sorry, Father. Just a little
> pre-wedding jitters.

>   PETE (AS PRIEST)
> I understand, my son.

                    CAL
Let's get this show on the road.

                    FLO
Yeah, the horror show.

                    CAL
What?

                    FLO
Nothing.

                    PETE (AS PRIEST)
Are we ready? Let us begin. Love
goes back to the beginning of
time...

                    CAL
Just give us the short version.

                    PETE (AS PRIEST)
The short version?

                    CAL
You know, all the "I do's" and
such.

                    PETE (AS PRIEST)
Well, we must get a few things
straight first.

                    CAL
Straight? What do you mean?

                    PETE (AS PRIEST)
Do you love this woman?

                    CAL
You bet.

(CAL slaps her on the rear - or makes kissy lips)

                    PETE (AS PRIEST)
Do you love this man?

                    REMMY
I most certainly...

(CAL points his gun at her)

                    REMMY (CONT.)
Well...

                    CAL
Say it.

                    PETE (AS PRIEST)
I can not perform the ceremony
pointing a gun pointing at the
bride.

                    CAL
How about I point it at you
instead?

                    PETE (AS PRIEST)
I suppose I could do it then.

                    CAL
Hurry it up. I ain't got all night.

                    PETE (AS PRIEST)
Do you, Cal Capone...

(SADIE enters and her ghostly voice booms out)

                    SADIE
Cal Capone.

                    CAL
What was that?

                    JAQUE
What was what?

                    FLO
I didn't hear anything.

                    PETE (AS PRIEST)
Take this woman...

                    SADIE
Kill this woman...

                    CAL
Who is that? Who said that?

                    JAQUE
Are you okay, Cal?

                    CAL
I swore I heard someone say...

                    PETE (AS PRIEST)
Shall we continue?

                         CAL
          The sooner we get out of here the
          better.

                         SADIE
          Get out of here!

                         CAL
          Hurry!

                         PETE (AS PRIEST)
          Do you Cal Capone...

                         SADIE
          Cal Capone.

                         CAL
          You said that already.

                         PETE (AS PRIEST)
          Take this woman...

                         SADIE
          Kill this woman...

                         PETE (AS PRIEST)
          Ruth Remmington.

                         SADIE
          Sadie Smithington!

                         CAL
          It's her!

                         FLO
          Who?

                         CAL
          Sadie!

                         SADIE
          Sadie!

                         CAL
          She's come back!

(SADIE approaches CAL. He can see her now. He backs away)

                         SADIE
          I've come for you, Cal!

                         CAL
          Please, Sadie. I didn't mean to
          kill you. It was an accident. It
          was Al's idea. I didn't want
          anything to do with it.

                         SADIE
          You must pay!

                         PETE (AS PRIEST)
          Are you okay, my son?

                         CAL
          Can't you see her?!

                         FLO
          We can't see anything.

                         CAL
          It's her! Sadie! She's come back
          to haunt me.

                         JAQUE
          You're nuts, man.

(JAQUE and FLO exit)

                         SADIE
          I've come to drive you nuts!

                         CAL
          Please, no!

                         SADIE
          I will be with you every day of
          your life.

                         CAL
          No!

                         SADIE
          I will never leave you. Like you
          promised me. We'd never be
          apart. But you betrayed me!

                         CAL
          Please, Sadie. I'll do anything you
          say. Just leave me alone.

                         SADIE
          You must never marry again!

                    CAL
          I won't. I won't.

                    SADIE
          You must never ruin a woman's life
          like you ruined mine.

                    CAL
          Never again. Remmy, the wedding's
          off!

                    REMMY
          You mean it?

                    SADIE
          Tell her you mean it!

                    CAL
          I mean it!

                    SADIE
          Promise her!

                    CAL
          I promise!

                    SADIE
          I don't think you mean it.

(This is a line that isn't in the original play they have
been performing so BENDER/CAL is confused)

                    BENDER/CAL
          Huh?

                    SADIE
          I call upon my minions to seek
          revenge on all who have harmed
          me... starting with you, Cal.

                    BENDER
          What the... what are you talking
          about?

(Moaning is heard and creatures enter the stage. JIMMY,
MAYA, VERA and any other actors available are dressed as
zombies. JAQUE and FLO are creatures as well if a quick
change is possible using masks, etc. They all slowly lumber
toward CAL/BENDER)

                    BENDER (CONT.)
          Hey! What's going on?

                                              (CONTINUED)

                         SADIE
               Attack, my minions! Attack!

(BENDER screams and runs off. The PRINCIPAL comes up on
stage)

                         PRINCIPAL
               What are you all doing? This isn't
               supposed to happen.

(Principal turns to audience. The creatures start
approaching him from behind)

                         PRINCIPAL (CONT.)
               I'm so sorry everyone. Obviously
               we have some students playing a
               prank on us tonight. We'll have to
               end our performance a bit early...

                         CREATURES
               Wedgie... wedgie...

                         PRINCIPAL
               What... what are you talking
               about...

(PRINCIPAL turns and realizes the CREATURES are heading
toward him)

                         CREATURES
               Wedgie... wedgie!

                         PRINCIPAL
               No! No! Stop this instant! No
               wedgies!

(PRINCIPAL runs off and CREATURES follow except for JIMMY,
HARM, PENNY and BRAD)

                         BRAD
               This is so fun!

(BRAD acts like a creature now and follows. PENNY hugs HARM
and JIMMY)

                         PENNY
               Thanks. I gotta see this.

(PENNY runs off)

                         HARM
               That was totally awesome, Jimmy.

(HARM gives him a punch on the arm and puts on her mask
again to join the minions)

                    JIMMY
          Hey... uh... Harm?

                    HARM
          Yeah?

                    JIMMY
          Doesn't the play end with a kiss?

                    HARM
          You wish.

(HARM gets in to creature mode and turns to him)

                    HARM (CONT.)
          Wedgie... wedgie....

(JIMMY runs off and HARM lumbers after him)

ACT II SCENE 4 BACK IN DETENTION

(HARM, JIMMY, PENNY, BENDER, BRAD, BIFF, JASMINE and
MADELINE all are sitting in detention. PRINCIPAL enters)

                    BRAD
          I think that was the best show
          we've ever done here.

                    MADELINE
          The school loved it.

                    JASMINE
          Especially the new ending.

                    BRAD
          The rest of the school wants to see
          it now. They want an encore
          performance.

                    JASMINE
          I'd totally do it... if the
          principal would let us.

                    MADELINE
          Fat chance.

                                                  (CONTINUED)

                    HARM
Speak of the devil.

                  PRINCIPAL
Brad, Madeline and Jasmine. You
are not in detention. Please
leave.

                  JASMINE
We're here to support are fellow
actors.

                  MADELINE
They don't deserve more detention.

                    BRAD
This is wrong Principal Paine.

                  PRINCIPAL
You want wrong? Fine then. You
three have detention now too.

                    BIFF
That's not fair.

                  PRINCIPAL
I'm not here to be fair. I'm here
to teach you all something. This
is my school and my rules. When you
walk through those doors you're
expected to follow my lead...
otherwise there will be chaos.

                    HARM
Your lead? What kind of leader are
you? I can't follow a leader who is
corrupt, selfish and vindictive.
What kind of example is that?

                  PRINCIPAL
An example that will get you a lot
farther in life than the road
you're headed down.

                   JIMMY
I would rather go down any road
with these people... but never any
road you're on. I don't think you
want us following too close behind
at the rear anyway.

(All the students laugh. PRINCIPAL adjusts his pants
nervously)

PRINCIPAL
You will all write "I will not give
Principal Paine a wedgie" 5,000
times. I want you all to say it for
me so I know it's clear.

ALL
I will give Principal Paine a
wedgie.

PRINCIPAL
No! "I will not..."

(JIMMY stands up on his chair. Dramatic music can begin
playing that builds as the scene builds)

JIMMY
I will give Principal Paine a
wedgie.

(HARM stands up on her chair)

HARM
I will give Principal Paine a
wedgie.

(PENNY stands up on her chair)

PENNY
I will give Principal Paine a
wedgie.

PRINCIPAL
Stop this at once! All of you back
in your seats!

(Rest of the group stands on their chairs)

ALL
I will give Principal Paine a
wedgie!

(PRINCIPAL throws detention slips at them)

PRINCIPAL
All of you get detention for the
rest of your lives!

JIMMY
And we will haunt you the rest of
yours... because are the Ghosts of
Detention! We are the Wedgie Club!

(PRINCIPAL leaves in anger and lights fade as they all stand
proudly together)

                    JIMMY
          Carpe wedgie, gang. Carpe wedgie.

                    HARM
          Seize the wedgie?

(They all laugh as lights fade to black)

(Lights come up on a giant backdrop that looks like a
chalkboard. On the sides are written "I will give Principal
Paine a wedgie" over and over in different
handwriting. Then in the middle is written the following
monologue by JIMMY. His voice is heard as the lights reveal
the board)

                    JIMMY
          Sometimes doing the wrong thing
          feels so right. There are bad
          people who use good rules and
          corrupt them. That's when you stand
          up and say, "I will give you a
          wedgie. You don't deserve to lead.
          You have ruined your chance because
          you twist the rules for your own
          gain and hurt others in the
          process. It does not matter how
          right the rule is... You manage to
          make it wrong. So we say to you,
          sir... and all others like you...
          you deserve a wedgie."

OPTIONAL ENDING SCENE

(Lights come back up and JIMMY finishes writing the words on
the board. Everyone is gone and JIMMY backs up to get a
good look at what he wrote. But then HARM returns)

                    HARM
          Hey, Jimmy.

                    JIMMY
          Returning to the scene of the
          crime?

                    HARM
          I have a question for you.

                          JIMMY
               Sure... what is it?

                          HARM
               Doesn't the play end with a kiss?

                          JIMMY
               Well... uh... I...

                          HARM
               You're cute.

     (HARM kisses JIMMY and lights fade to black)

                        END OF PLAY

CAST OF CHARACTERS

Small cast size (speaking roles): 5 male, 6 female - 11
total

Large cast size (speaking roles): 26 total

****

Setting is a 1980's High School

****

Detention Cast

JIMMY (also plays AL CAPONE)

HARM (also plays FLO)

PENNY (also plays REMMY)

BIFF (also plays JAQUE)

BENDER (also plays CAL CAPONE)

TINY (can play other characters later or can be doubled with
JIMMY if cast is limited)

PRINCIPAL

COACH (can be doubled with PRINCIPAL if cast is limited)

GERTY/GERTRUDE

MADELINE (also plays MAYA)

                                            (CONTINUED)

JASMINE (also plays SADIE the ghost)

BRITNEY (also plays VERA)

****

Setting in the past: Roaring 1920's

****

Bonnie and Clyde Cast

Detective 1 - PETE played by BRAD

Detective 2 - played by JIMMY or another actor

HENRY - played by BIFF or another actor

MAYA - played by MADELINE

****

Ghost Hunters of Route 666 Cast

REMMY played by PENNY

PETE is played by BRAD

HARM plays FLO

JAQUE/JAQUE played by BIFF

MAYA is plays by MADELINE

****

Seeing Beyond with Maya Fantasma

MAYA (played by MADELINE): The MAYA who can talk to the dead.

SADIE (played by JASMINE): The dead person who needs to find her killer.

JAQUE (played by BIFF): Boyfriend of Vera

VERA (played by BRITNEY): The person SADIE wants to warn JAQUE about.

ANNOUNCER (can be prerecorded) - played by PETE or JIMMY or another actor

****

(CONTINUED)

Hysterical History of Great Depression

PETE played by BRAD

BAILIFF played by a new actor ideally but can also be played by BENDER or BIFF

AL CAPONE played by JIMMY

MADELINE, HARM, BIFF, BENDER and JASMINE can be crowd if other actors are not available - *Woman 1 and 2 - women in the crowd of the court, *Man 1 and 2 - men in the crowd of the court, Child - male or female - kid who got a bicycle from Capone

VERA (played by BRITNEY)

TRANSCRIPTIONIST (could double with VERA if actors are limited?)

RUTHERFORD - played by new actor ideally or by BENDER or BIFF

*These parts can be combined to one actor. Additional actors may be in the crowd.

****

Creepy Corpse Cast of Characters

REMMY played by PENNY

PETE/PRIEST played by BRAD

FLO played by HARM

JAQUE played by BIFF

MAYA played by MADELINE

SADIE played by JASMINE

**SAM and SALLY: Other patrons in optional scene (new actor)

SIMON: Confused customer (played by new actor or JIMMY)

KID: Another confused customer (can be same KID as Hysterical History scene)

**COP - new actor in optional scene

CAL CAPONE - played by BENDER

**DRUNK - new actor in optional scene

26315578R00072

Made in the USA
Middletown, DE
24 November 2015